PRAISE FOR RA

"Living Fearlessly is full of wisdom and very accessible. I think it will totally hit the spot for those seeking more out of life."

— NICOLA BIRD, FOUNDER OF A LITTLE PEACE OF MIND

"I love Living Fearlessly because it's subtle. On the surface I found it practical with lots of good stories and metaphors and I enjoyed finding out more and connecting with your story. Whilst reading, I felt myself growing calm and joining you on the inner journey. Although I intellectually knew what you were talking about, a deeper feeling crept up on me like a warm blanket invisibly wrapping itself around me as the feeling of your words took me to a deeper place. I let it effortlessly weave its magic whilst I read. I look forward to recommending this book to friends and clients."

— GILLIAN FOX, CLARITY COACH

"I love books which work on the reader at different levels, and that is what Rachel has created. On the conscious level, 'Living Fearlessly' is a good read about one person's journey of discovery and making sense of how to effortlessly live without fear. On the unconscious level, magic happens without the reader even necessarily being aware of what happened!

Definitely a book to be highly recommended and well worth checking out sooner rather than later."

— KEITH BLAKEMORE-NOBLE AKA THE CONFIDENCE ALCHEMIST™, HYPNOTIST AND PHOBIA EXPERT.

"Life can be easy when we understand where fear comes from. There's no need to 'face our fears', or to suffer a constant, underlying feeling of anxiety. What Rachel Henke shares in 'Living Fearlessly,' goes beyond self-help and how-to advice and explores the inside-out paradigm of how the mind works. Don't be fooled by the simplicity of the idea, the results of looking at life through this lens will change your relationship with 'fear'. Forever."

— CATHY PRESLAND, TRANSFORMATIVE LEADERSHIP COACH

"I love how relatable the book is and how naturally Rachel helps us understand how we can be fearless without having to confront our fears!"

— ROBIN TAFFIN, BUSINESS AND EXECUTIVE COACH

LIVING FEARLESSLY

A SIMPLE GUIDE TO LIVING THE LIFE YOU WANT, WITHOUT THE NEED TO FIGHT YOUR FEARS, BREAK THROUGH BLOCKS, OR BECOME A BATTLE HARDENED WARRIOR.

RACHEL HENKE

RACHEL HENKE GLOBAL LTD.

To my daughters, Amy and Ella. You are beautiful, fearless souls who inspire me. This is for you.

CONTENTS

INTRODUCTION

LIVING FEARLESSLY turns everything you think you already know about fear, inside out.

As you read this book I invite you to look for truth.

I encourage you to look for what **you** see. Don't take my word for it.

The book is a description of how life works, not a prescription for how to live.

Test the ideas in this book and listen for your own inner voice of wisdom to guide you.

To begin living fearlessly, all that's required is to be open to hearing something new. The content of this book may be unlike anything you've read before. There are no complex exercises to complete or 'working on yourself' to do.

Relax and read this book as if it were fiction. Let the words wash over you. Listen for the space between the text. Allow your own insights to soak in. What does that quiet voice inside of you whisper as you read? Your fearless intuition will begin speaking to you and you'll experience your own insights.

Give yourself permission to act on what you feel naturally motivated to do, rather than what you think you should do. This is how we set ourselves free.

You can break the rules. There are no rules anyway. We've made them all up.

The essence of living fearlessly is knowing we're already beautifully equipped to live an incredible life of freedom. All that's required to live fearlessly is to be alive. If you qualify … read on!

I do hope you'll join me on this journey. Once you begin living fearlessly I promise you that life will never feel like a battle again.

PART I

THE FEARLESS PARADIGM

1

MY FEARLESS SHIFT

Everything we have learned about fear is wrong. Transformation occurs when we stop trying to fight fear and instead allow our fearless intuition to guide us. We are already fully equipped to live an amazing, fearless life. When we wake up to how our human experience is created; fear, anxiety and stress dissolve effortlessly. When we're aware of our fearless intuition we're naturally motivated, resilient and confident.

This is the complete antithesis of what we read in most books about fear. Personal development usually involves conquering, fighting resistance and becoming a fearless warrior. In this book you'll discover the universal principles which reveal our true fearless nature. You'll learn how to trust your intuition so you can live fearlessly. I must warn you. We're unable to plug ourselves back into the 'matrix,' once we see the truth of how the human experience works. You'll never be the same again.

Hello, I'm Rachel. I'm a best-selling author, Transformation

Coach and the Founder of Living Fearlessly. I'm also a recovering self-development junkie and spiritual seeker. A couple of years ago I stumbled across a revolutionary understanding, which completely changed my life. Once seen, the way we see the world changes, forever. I call it the fearless paradigm because it facilitates a paradigm shift.

I was five years old when my mother died on the operating table. After that I moved around a lot. Later I experienced acute anxiety which I tried to control with varying degrees of success. At the age of sixteen, I developed panic attacks and as a result I seemed to always be searching for a way to manage my fears. I'm sharing my personal story in the hopes it will help you to see that tragic events don't need to define us. We all have everything we need to be happy and successful, no matter what's happened in the past, or may happen in the future. This is what we'll be exploring together in 'Living Fearlessly.'

Following my mother's death I lived with my grandmother in Northern England, until she died of cancer. It was a slow, painful death and I watched her suffer quietly over a period of several years. My most terrifying, dark thoughts of Nina dying, and me left alone in the world without her, materialised. I adored a television programme about a little gypsy girl who lived with her grandmother in a caravan. It was them against the world and that's how I imagined us.

Nina was in her late seventies and unwell so she didn't venture out a great deal. I had a lot of freedom to run wild. I was very independent and would spend hours racing about the grounds of our large Georgian flat, leaping off high walls with my cousins. Another favourite pastime was whiling away the hours curled up in a red leather armchair by a huge window overlooking the big circular driveway. I immersed myself in the secret world of Enid Blyton or C.S Lewis and I knew by the age of seven, I wanted to write books.

Nina would talk to me as if I was an adult so I matured early. She'd read sordid Catherine Cookson tales to me late at night in bed. Most of my family were keen readers and I grew up thinking everyone read every day. We'd visit the library weekly without fail. Although I loved the stories about the turbulent world Catherine Cookson's characters inhabited, it probably wasn't reassuring for me.

For years after Nina's death I felt guilty because I thought I hadn't done enough and her dying was in some way my fault. By the time she passed away on Easter, 'Good Friday,' I was secretly relieved not to have to watch her wrestle with her pain anymore. And then I felt even more guilty. Have you ever had a thought, and then hidden it from others because you felt wracked by guilt? I was just ten or eleven and I never told anyone about my secret shame. It was a heavy weight to bear and I carried it with me like a loaded backpack. Such is the nature of guilt. It's irrational and can suck us in like a riptide. Before we know it, we're cast out into turbulent seas and can't find our way back to calm waters. I had no idea my thoughts weren't real. I thought I must be a very wicked girl and had little confidence in myself. This is why I feel so compelled to share this revolutionary understanding about how we experience our reality through our thoughts.

My father, Percy, was born in 1939 on the island of Jersey, shortly before the Nazis occupied the Channel Islands. He joined the navy at age sixteen to travel the world. The only memory I have of the day my mother died, is of him wearing a white sheepskin coat. Head in hands, he sat on a chair, sobbing like an inconsolable child. To see your father sob isn't something I wish on anyone. I have no memory at all of what followed but I've been told, he struggled to come to terms with her death. He left his job as a top performing salesman and returned to sea to work on the oil rigs.

Before Nina died, we moved to Oxfordshire to live with my auntie. By this time Nina was extremely ill. Shortly after she died, my father returned and my moving from house to house and school to school commenced. My father and I moved around, staying with various friends whilst he tried to make ends meet. He was by this time a self-employed salesman and his income was very unpredictable. Sometimes we'd be shaking the whisky bottle, rummaging for coins to pay for my bus fare and school lunch.

This period was a nightmare for me. I'd moved from my new primary school to high school as well as moving to live with a 'friend' of mine who soon began to resent our presence. She spread lies and incited others to bully me at school. At the end of the school day when it was time to leave, I'd go back to her house and she'd pick fights with me there too. There were many evenings in that house when I'd be fraught with terror, imagining my father would have an accident and not come back for me. He liked being at the pub and in those days it was quite common to drink and drive. I would work myself up into a state and wouldn't be able to relax until I heard his car roll into the driveway. Feeling fearful and unsafe had become the norm for me by then.

Prior to this we lived in a room over a pub for a while. It was pretty rowdy and there were no other kids about, but there were some benefits. I'd get first dibs on all of the juke box tracks as soon as it was updated. I spent many happy hours singing along to the latest hits. This is a great example of how no matter how sad we feel, we're only ever one thought away from a new, happy one. We can experience joy at any moment, even in the midst of difficult times. It's a beautiful truth which is reliable because it's how our experience always works.

On the worst days I would beg my dad to let me go on the road with him instead of going to school. Mostly he'd pack me off on the bus, but now and then when he recognised I was in a particularly dark mood, he'd take me with him. We'd knock on doors, trying to sell luxury, embroidered blankets. I adored my dad and one of my happiest memories is sitting with him in his brown Simca, chomping on a huge pancake roll from the chip shop. Isn't it comforting how the most simple interactions often bring us the most contentment? We often don't realise how special they were until later. Finally my dad must have seen how miserable I was or perhaps he simply ran out of money. He then decided we would go to Jersey where his mother lived. I'd only met my other grandmother a couple of times but she'd regularly sent me gifts by post and was thrilled to welcome us.

As you may imagine I was relieved to be out of my 'friend's' house, and we set off on what felt like an extremely long journey by train and ferry to Jersey. My nan smothered us in love. Such was the contrast to my previous lone ranger style emotional life, my ability to let someone love me so demonstratively, must have temporarily shut down. I felt suffocated by her need to drown me in love. I chose to go and live with distant cousins who were then childless and keen to have me. Not surprisingly their enthusiasm soon wore off and I became the referee of their almost daily arguments. I'm happy to say I soon grew close to my nan and we had a wonderful, loving relationship right up until her death.

As a young woman I went for counselling, hypnotherapy and acupuncture. They helped with my anxiety a little but I suspected the answer was not to be found in trawling through my past. I'm naturally optimistic so I decided I would try and fix myself. Thus commenced my self-improvement journey. I've since read hundreds of books about mindset, psychology and self-development.

From a young age I yearned to travel and always had a real sense of adventure. I did things other people found courageous. At age seventeen, I left home and I left a secure job with a funded college place. I was a fearless rebel. I can see now I wasn't truly fearless. I was running away from ordinary life because I found it too overwhelming and scary. The idea of working in a bank for the rest of my life, terrified me. Often it's the everyday, the ordinary things that fill us with fear.

MY ANXIETY DISAPPEARED

As a result of understanding the fearless principles outlined in this book, my anxiety disappeared. It's difficult to put into words just how profound this change in my experience has been. It feels as though I have access to true mental freedom for the first time in my life. Reading hundreds of personal development books didn't cure my anxiety, understanding these principles did. My habitual pattern of future fearful thinking which used to spin around in my mind most days, occurs much less frequently. And when it does, it dissolves quicker. There are similar life changing shifts in my clients and colleagues who are gaining this understanding. I'll share more about how we all have the capacity for anxiety and worry to drop away effortlessly, later in the book.

Recently I worked with a client who is a University Professor and Hypnotherapist. When we began working together she was very stressed and anxious about her relationship and her career.

During our first session she experienced what she called a 'eureka moment.' There was a sudden shift in her thoughts and perception of her situation. This was something she said she hadn't experienced in all of the therapies and self-help she'd tried. Within a week of starting working with me, she shared that her world had become more positive, she was engaging in work again and being incredibly productive. Over time she became a do-er rather than a thinker and was so much happier and at ease. She began saying yes to all kinds of opportunities, and even appeared in a T.V documentary, sharing her expertise. In the past she'd stopped herself from doing things she wanted to do, for fear of getting it wrong. She became care free and started to go with the flow. Her anxious mind settled and finally she felt free of self-doubt. This is one example of how an insight can shift our experience and create effortless change.

I haven't been trying to work hard on myself as I used to, which is the best part for me. I've experienced this increased mental freedom and peace of mind simply by understanding how my mind works. Transformation occurs through experiencing insights which shift our perception of what's happening in our world.

I now understand the human experience much better due to my immersion in this transformative paradigm. I see clearly why one person regards something as scary, whilst another is unperturbed by the same situation. Feeling the fear and doing it anyway isn't necessary to create what we want.

We all spend less time thinking about certain things or perhaps don't think about them at all. The areas we worry about less, don't seem as fearsome because we don't obsess about them. It's counterintuitive to most of what we've been taught about overcoming fear.

I SAW SOMETHING NEW IN THE FORM OF AN INSIGHT

Like all life changing events, we don't usually see them coming and so it was with this one. It snuck up on me. I signed up for an online course with a British coach, Nicola Bird. I began looking in the new direction she was pointing. I'll never forget on one of the early calls she was talking about the Three Principles of Mind, Consciousness and Thought and how understanding them transforms our experience of life. I don't remember the words she used but I remember the beautiful feeling. I glimpsed something new about the nature of doing what I'm inspired to do, versus what I think I should do. Now I recognise this as an 'insight,' or 'realisation.' I was hooked. Have you ever noticed how sometimes you know something in your gut, but you can't logically put your finger on why it makes sense? That's how I felt. It's the feeling of intuition always available to guide us. We'll be exploring this more deeply as we take this 'Living Fearlessly,' journey together.

For years I'd been trying to access the feeling of being in flow more often. I have a fascination with productivity and creativity. This understanding is the missing piece of the puzzle. I suspected I'd stumbled across something which explained how humans tick in a profound but simple way. This took me upstream of the strategies and techniques I'd come across in all of my studying and seeking. I said, 'Well that sounds wonderful if it's true.' And Nicola replied, 'I don't want to convince you. Look in this direction and see what you see for yourself.' This alone was a revelation to me.

I was used to being spoon fed strategies by teachers trying to convince me that if I had only taken the action prescribed in their magical system I would be having the same results as them. I had grown jaded because I modelled them but often didn't get the same outcome. The variable is in each of us being different and showing up to a completely unique set of circumstances at any given time. It's common sense but the online business space is crowded with experts teaching others how to be leaders in their field. The idea is to motivate them to follow their system so they can essentially be exactly like them. Oh the irony ...

'Something is rotten in the state of Denmark,' the famous line from William Shakespeare's, Hamlet, comes to mind as I write this. I'd spotted this incongruence early on in my entrepreneurial journey. I shifted to teaching people to find their own way, not to copy mine. However, people often feel the fear of failing and seek to model another. They long to believe it's a guarantee it will work the same way for them. It's not.

And yet, having an awareness of all of this, I still stumbled about for the next year trying to fit these mysterious three principles into my current world view. Not content with an online course I enrolled for private coaching so I could really get to the bottom of this. I'm not one to dabble. If this was the way to experience more happiness and to help others to transform on a deeper level than the usual 'managing your state,' techniques, I was hungry to know more.

It seemed the logical next step. And that's the point where we left logic at the door and began a transformational journey of exploring the true nature of how humans operate. I saw that like most people, I'd been living in a misunderstanding of reality for most of my life. In all of my years of reading, learning, seeking and sharing various mindset, psychological and spiritual understandings, I'd never found anything which explained how life works in the simple way these principles do.

Like many truth seekers, I'd read lots of books and experienced insights over the years. My fascination with the spiritual nature of life deepened when I arrived in Jerusalem on my eighteenth birthday. Years later, I read 'The Power Of Now' by Eckhart Tolle but I couldn't hear what he was saying in a practical way which I could apply to my life prior to gaining this new understanding, I realised I was still living as if my work was one thing but my deeper connection to inspiration felt elusive. I found this very frustrating as I wanted to experience more of it.

For anyone with a God phobia let me be clear: I'm not referring to religious observance. I'm talking about being aware of our connection to the creative intelligence behind life. This is the intelligence which transforms bare fields into blankets of blazing red poppies. It's the same intelligence which effortlessly transports the blood through our veins, no matter what our personal beliefs. People often have strange ideas about what this means. When I spoke about this intelligence behind life on my internet radio show some years ago, the episodes were taken off air because they were considered anti-religious.

On the scientific end of the spectrum, even world renowned

theoretical physicist, Dr. Stephen Hawking said, 'You cannot understand the glories of the Universe without believing there is some supreme power behind it.'

Coaches sometimes talk about being spiritually aligned with business, but practice a completely 'outside in' approach to life. The underlying message is usually that we'll be happy and successful when we reach our destination. This leads to confused thinking and often results in people worrying they're not 'good enough.' The innocent implication is we think we're unable to be happy until we reach the arbitrary goal which often revolves around an income figure.

What happens when the few reach their magical figure is they're then advised to set a higher one and it starts all over again in the quest to reach 'the next level.' Where we are now is never enough. And this might be okay if people were happy doing it. In reality, when I talk to business owners and other high achievers, no matter what level of business or income they're at, they usually talk longingly about the future. They've been conditioned to think they need to reach their goal to be happy. We don't even know we're doing it until someone shows us a different way of being.

Underpinning it all are usually feelings of unworthiness and a desperation to reach a destination which by it's very nature we can never reach. This means we're in a trap of never allowing ourselves to be content for more than a few moments. When we live in this way we miss out on the joy of being alive which we could be experiencing every single day! How sad is that? When we wake up to what's really going on, it's a huge paradigm shift.

The majority of people never get anywhere near their magical money figure and spend most of their time stressing, worrying and trying to figure out how they can reach it so they can stop worrying. They believe they will then be happy.

It's a proven prescription for unhappiness and suffering. This isn't theory. We only have to look around us to spot it in action. This was me in my first business. I worked with hundreds of people desperately hoping to reach their destination which would supposedly mean they could be free. Talk about a thought-created virtual reality. We had no idea we were already free. In the next chapter we'll explore the inside-out nature of life. It helps us to see how feeling unworthy is simply another side effect of the big misunderstanding of how our experience works.

When I share this understanding, I'm often struck by how people initially assume they've heard it before. It sounds familiar because I'm pointing to what we already know in terms of how life works.

It's a description, not a prescription. It's easy to miss the deeper impact of seeing beyond our old ideas. Some of my clients have studied psychology but initially have no sense of the depth of what I'm pointing to. Having certifications and letters after our names often means we use our bodies to carry our heads around. Those who pride themselves on their intelligence, tend to over-think, and spend hours each day lost in busy thoughts. In many cases a powerful intellect gets in the way. It won't allow us to sit in the unknown to be open to glimpse something new. It feels too scary.

When we're used to thinking we're in control and need to be in control to be safe, the unknown feels like a very fearful place. When we have a 'control freak,' tendency, the unknown doesn't look full of exciting possibilities and opportunities. It looks terrifying because we see to what extent we're not in control, and never were.

We have a natural tendency to make order of new information we receive by attempting to fit it into what we already know. This is exactly what I tried to do. I see this happening with many of my clients. I liken it to each of us having a mental inbox where all kinds of information lands at all times of the day. We then attempt to fit each new entry into an appropriate file so it's not whizzing about our mind in a chaotic fashion. We don't like open loops and unsolved problems so we want them filed immediately. That's because we think we can stop thinking about it and enjoy peace of mind.

The problem with operating in this way is we're very likely to miss new, fresh and important ideas which as yet have no file created to receive them. In this transformation conversation we call these wonderful glimpses of truth, insights. I encourage you to be exposed to the ideas in this book with an open mind. Be ready to see something new. When we attempt to fit the new ideas and insights, into existing methodologies, philosophies or systems, we burn through our mental bandwidth quickly. What I mean by this is when we try to figure something out with our intellect and we don't understand it, we quickly lose clarity. Our mental process becomes foggy. Let's open up a beautiful new space and be open to seeing something new which can transform your state of mind and experience of life.

Whether you're interested in growing a better business or career, feeling less anxious, making more money, having more impact, being more productive, creating a new project, having better relationships or simply enjoying life more, there's something here for you. All we ever need to do is allow ourselves to settle down mentally to see it. This understanding seems to reveal itself to us the more we make ourselves available to it in a playful manner.

In my online fearless classes I invite participants to listen to the content like music. As this is a book I invite you to read it like fiction. When you read fiction you're probably pretty relaxed and not desperately trying to get something from the story. Instead, you can sit back and enjoy the journey. As with a fictional plot, things are often not what they seem and it's the same when we begin to uncover our fearless nature and follow the path that unfolds.

––––––

HERE'S A SUMMARY OF THE KEY POINTS IN THIS CHAPTER:

- Past experiences and our 'old story' do not define us. We already have everything we need to be happy and successful no matter what's happened in the past.
- Personal transformation happens through experiencing our own insights. We're more open to insight once we understand how the system works. It doesn't require us to work on ourselves.
- Feeling the fear and doing it anyway isn't necessary to create what we want.
- Read this book like fiction; allow it to wash over you without trying to intellectually understand every point.
- The more we look in this direction, the more we see.

There's an 'insight' space below to journal any new thoughts that come through as you read:

_____

_____

_____

Let's now take the next step together to explore the inside-out nature of life.

2

THE INSIDE-OUT NATURE OF LIFE

I 'll refer to the inside-out nature of life often in this book. I want to share what I mean so you'll know what to look for as we travel together on our living fearlessly journey. When I first came across the understanding about how our experience of life unfolds, I was confused. Once I understood the inside-out nature of life, my world opened up and my vision was clear.

I could see for certain my happiness wasn't dependent upon my circumstances. Although in some areas it looked as though it surely was, such as believing the sun made me happy. I used to believe I was happier because the sun was shining. Now I understand it's impossible for circumstances to make me happy. Happiness is an inside-out job. Happiness can only ever come from inside.

Think about it; the sun shines and one person has happy thoughts and feels happy in the moment. Another person prayed for rain to relieve the drought and feels desperate at the sight of the sun. Wellbeing, like happiness, comes from inside us, it's not 'out there.' I spent thirty years on a deep spiritual journey. It's crazy when I think about it. I studied mindset, psychology, spirituality and metaphysics, all in a quest to find the secret of happiness. I wasn't studying these topics to become an expert in them, I was studying them to make myself feel better. And to be honest I didn't feel much better at all.

I was trying to fix myself, because I believed I must be broken in some way. The underlying message we hear from the personal development world is that, 'We're not okay as we are.' We are encouraged to believe we need something 'out there' in order to be complete. We'll be fixed. We'll be complete. Our life will be perfect.

Be mindful not to dismiss what I'm saying as one of those spiritual philosophies where money doesn't make you happy. This isn't what I mean at all. I think it is great to make money and I love helping people to do so. We want to have impact, and we need resources to do so. We also want to have material stuff in the world. We want to live comfortably and be able to provide for our families. But the misunderstanding of our wellbeing, happiness and success, coming from something 'out there,' is the source of much suffering and confusion. Because wellbeing, happiness and success don't come from 'out there.' They come from in there; from inside of us. And once you see that, you can see everything.

I used to believe I needed a certain number of clients or my books needed to be at a certain rank on Amazon for me to be content. It shows up in all areas of our lives. A common belief is that we need our relationship to be a certain way in order for us to be fulfilled. When we have expectations of how someone should behave, we get caught up in this delusion and it creates intense discomfort.

I was deep in the misunderstanding of my happiness depending on a specific set of circumstances. What this does is suspend us in a web of uncertainty. We feel dependent on either someone or something, to fill us up and make us happy. As it turns out we have absolutely no control over anyone. Many get wise to this and so it seems like a good idea to go to work on ourselves. We may have adopted beliefs such as, 'I can control the world by controlling my thoughts.' It's a never ending journey, because we can never get there no matter how determined we are. There's always one more negative thought to control. Once we see the inside-out nature of life, controlling ceases to make sense. We no longer need to try to manage the universe, which frees up a huge amount of time, energy and space. This discovery brings relief and hope to those of us who have battled with our fearful thoughts for years. It's enough to wake up to the universal truth of our experience never coming from anything outside of us, even if it looks as though it does.

We can move beyond the idea of needing our world to be a certain way in order to feel happy. Instead, we're open to some fresh, new thought coming through about our situation. In the Three Principles field, this capacity for new thought, is known as insight. The content of our insights is unique to each of us. The wisdom which can pour through our minds, gives us fresh perspective on our lives in a way which other people's pre-packaged advice can't do. Other people's ideas can be very helpful but they're not tailored for our personal experience in the way our own insights are. They're rarely transformative because one size doesn't fit all. When we catch a glimpse of space around our entrenched beliefs it creates the possibility for limitless and effortless transformation.

WE LIVE IN THE FEELING OF OUR THINKING 100% OF THE TIME

Our experience only ever comes from our thought created perception in any given moment. This is 100% of the time, with no exceptions. The thoughts we have in the moment, create our feelings. We live in the feeling of our thinking. And this means all of the time; in every minute. Our thoughts always create our feelings. And this is contrary to most people's beliefs. It's not uncommon to believe your feelings create your thoughts.

Here's how Michael Neill, one of my mentors in the Three Principles field, describes how our thoughts create our feelings:

'We live in a world of thought, but we think we live in a world of external experience. The mind does not work like a camera - the mind works like a projector. It's like in a movie. The projector of mind takes the film of thought and projects it onto the screen of consciousness. And it really looks like it's happening out there and we experience it in here and it's scary or it's exciting or it's awesome or it's terrible — but none of it is actually happening outside of our own minds ...'

An example of this is when we're watching a film. For as long as I can remember I've had an irrational fear of dinosaurs. Yes, I know; they're not real, they're not walking the earth so they can't hurt me. I've been reassured many times but I still feel the fear when I think about dinosaurs. I went to see the first Jurassic Park when it premiered. Perhaps I was practicing feeling the fear and doing it anyway. During most of the film I hid my face in my hands and occasionally peeked through my fingers. Even though I knew it was only a film, I still felt afraid. But on a deeper level I also knew there weren't any dinosaurs in the cinema and the experience would soon be over. The difference when we feel fear in everyday situations is, we don't have the awareness of our experience being like watching a scary film. We live in the feeling of our thoughts all of the time, but it's easier to spot when we're watching a film. We mistakenly believe we're experiencing the film and the dinosaurs are really out to get us.

With this inside-out understanding, we naturally free ourselves from our dependency on any set of magic circumstances we think we must have in order to experience wellbeing. We already have everything we need, available within us, no matter which film we're watching. After being immersed in this fearless paradigm, underpinned by the Three Principles of Mind, Consciousness and Thought, I wondered, 'Why don't more people know about this? The inside-out nature of life is the real secret.'

It's not been all joyful enlightenment for me. I'm definitely still human. There were days where I felt bewildered as it was such a disruption in my habitual thought patterns. In its wake was left either huge inspiration or immense confusion as to what my next step would be. When our world view shifts, in a dramatic way, it feels like the ground moves beneath our feet. Michael Neill, calls this 'Shifting The Foundations,' and I've found it to be a very accurate description of the experience of transformation.

In some ways I felt more sure footed and safer than I ever recall feeling in my life. In others, the unknown had never looked more unknown to me. My fearful thinking began to gradually unravel as I saw my thoughts aren't real and so it no longer made sense to try to manage or control them. After years of trying to meditate and practice positive thinking, this effortless shift to standing on firmer ground was weirdly unsettling for me. I found myself wondering if it's okay to feel this okay. Shouldn't I be worrying about something? I no longer felt the need to micro-manage my experience, try to fix myself or to help others fix themselves. None of us are broken so what would be the point?

WE ALL HAVE ACCESS TO OUR OWN WISDOM WELL

What was I going to do with all of my time? Being a bit of a productivity geek, my first thought was how many hours of our lives we can save when we drop the obsession with constantly improving ourselves. Next, I realised I'd stumbled upon what I see as being the greatest productivity secret. We always have access to fresh wisdom. This may sound too simple. It's easy to miss the significance. Imagine owning a spring water well. For your entire life you have unlimited access to draw as many buckets of delicious, cool spring water, as you require. Our wisdom is freely available to us in the same way but most of us have no idea we own a wisdom well. When we draw on our own wisdom, there's less desire to seek permission and advice from others on how to live our lives.

As we go deeper together into this understanding, my hope is you'll begin to get a feel for your own inner knowing and wisdom. This realisation alone increases our productivity. I felt like I received the magic bullet to getting more done without the usual stress. We are the magic bullet. When we trust we'll see what we need as we need it, there's no sense in overthinking and over preparing. This spontaneity frees up hours on the clock and gives us back our mental freedom. I began to notice, 99% of personal development directs us away from the truth. No wonder so many of us are working on ourselves with strategies and techniques but never really enjoy a long term, sustainable improvement.

We Are Already Enough

Self improvement, even though well intended, points us in the direction of seeing ourselves as not good enough as we are. If we already knew we were enough, why would we need to continuously self improve? Why would we constantly feel the need to work on ourselves? After thirty years of personal development, one day I woke up and realised if it really worked this way, I'd have a perfect life already. As it is we're all perfect in our true nature.

Following our own insights doesn't eliminate the need or desire to develop skills. When my daughter wanted to learn to drive I didn't tell her to be open to insight and to give my car a spin. Instead, I booked her some driving lessons. Wisdom often shows up in the form of good old fashioned, common sense. It's reassuring to know we all have access to it when our thoughts settle down for long enough for it to get through. Where my daughter's own wisdom can guide her is in how she shows up for her lessons and how present she is when learning the various techniques required to be a competent driver. When we know our experience is 100% thought created, it provides a new, safe environment for us to develop a skill. We can take it to the next level, or master a new skill with far less self critiquing and judgement than we may have experienced in the past.

The old saying, 'You can't look good and get better at the same time,' points to the benefit of having less on our minds about how we're doing, as we learn or practice a new skill.

We'll explore this in more detail further on in the book because one of the biggest benefits of understanding how our human operating system works is that it gives us access to more mental freedom or 'bandwidth.' This allows us to play a fearless game and to experiment in ways we might never have felt confident to even contemplate previously. This has certainly been the case for me and many of my clients and colleagues. I quickly understood intellectually that our experience is 100% thought created but I didn't know it on a deeper level for some time. If it's a life-changing insight, it may repeatedly show up in different guises after the initial shift.

I think I've got it and then I see it on a deeper level, again and again. It's been this way for me with one of my first insights of 'get out of your own way.' Prior to discovering this understanding of how the human experience really works, it was little more than an intellectually good idea for me. The fact we often get in our own way is something few of us would argue with. The truth that we can get out of our own way, effortlessly and consistently, is something which hadn't revealed itself to me in any practical fashion before.

And now I see this truth in many shapes and forms. When my mood is low, clarity feels elusive and out of reach. When I'm not overthinking things — otherwise known as a 'thought storm,' my next step looks simple and easy to take. It's a 'no brainer.'

TRUE FREEDOM HAS NOTHING TO DO WITH A CLOCK

It was some while before I fully grasped the truth of how our thoughts create our experience of reality 100% of the time. Once you know on a gut level that there are no exceptions to this rule it can feel quite uncomfortable. For one thing, my coaching began to shift along with my world view. I was in the middle of writing my second business book, *The Freedom Solution: More Perfect Clients & Profits In Less Time.* I'd developed a virtual coaching business based around helping my clients create a 'Freedom Business Model,' with premium services. This was going well but gradually I saw more about where true freedom comes from. And you might have guessed by now. I saw it's not in our business model or anything to do with a clock at all.

By the time the book launched, with a picture of a clock on the cover, I already knew I'd uncovered the greatest productivity secret. My clients were being sprinkled with the magic mind dust of the fearless understanding. The results were incredible. They'd come to me to help them to create their signature programmes and premium business model. In addition they were experiencing deep personal transformation.

There was no longer any adrenalin fuelled hype — just grounded wisdom and insights. They were being guided by their own fearless wisdom in their life and work, without having to do anything. It's already in them. I point them to how it works.

One of my clients shared how he felt himself opening up to the sense of so much more being possible. He reported part of his brain saying, 'Yes, of course I know that...' and yet in another part of his brain it was like a door opening and he felt a deep sense of letting go. Another client shared how our conversations helped move her into an anxiety-free place. She said she now has the confidence to take the steps and the next thing unfolds without anxiety, hard work and stress.

Meanwhile, my fearless journey continued. Richard Bandler, the co-creator of Neuro-Linguistic Programming (NLP), reportedly observed there are people all over the world stuck in the various stages of his personal development. This resonated with me deeply. The Freedom Solution was my transition book; the bridge between the old and the new paradigm. I had invested both the time and money to work with a high level mentor for several years, in order to gain the skills and mindset of premium coaching. The premium business building skills won't be wasted. The mindset element represents the old paradigm of self-empowerment and outdated techniques of trying to make things happen. Insight comes through mind shifts rather than mindset. I'm reminded of how people once believed the world was flat and so their whole world view supported it. Once the belief was exposed as a misunderstanding of reality, their world view shifted. Such is this new paradigm. It represents the latest understanding of how our experience of life works. An old understanding is helpful only until we see the truth. We can't unsee it. Working upstream of beliefs is transformative because we're operating in reality.

My paradigm shift represented quite a conundrum for me in terms of what I was going to do next. I didn't want to fuel people's addiction to projected goals and illusory plans, but what would I do instead? The bottom dropped out of my coaching model and required me to explore coaching and business transformation from a fresh perspective.

I knew I couldn't do my old work in the same way. Skill building is very useful, especially when a client has a grounding in this fearless understanding. They are less prone to get lost in their own fearful reality and are able to take more inspired action. This is incredibly helpful in business. But being part of the conspiracy which prods people's insecurities so they feel not good enough unless they do things 'the right way,' wasn't something I aspired to. I'd participated innocently as many of us have done. Sadly, this is the way most marketing works. In my new way of working, we blend strategy with the fearless principles. This is the real game changer. I coach my clients to integrate their insights with whatever action makes sense for what they want to create. This supports them to find 'their way' of doing business or navigating life's challenges with ease. When we know where to find our natural motivation, action is effortless. Living Fearlessly was born as a result of understanding the principles I point to in this book and companion website.

Finally I began to experience the kind of euphoria I'd been looking for, more of the time. Although it wasn't encased in a positivity bubble as I'd expected it to be. These days I also find myself able to watch the news without being depressed. I used to keep myself firmly cocooned in the positive. Law of attraction teachings and popular personal development texts, such as 'Think And Grow Rich,' the classic prosperity book by Napoleon Hill, encourage us to protect ourselves from negativity. It turns out that hiding away from reality isn't as useful as I previously thought. What's really useful is seeing we're already resilient enough to deal with reality in whatever shape it comes at us. This is the core of what I mean by uncovering our true fearless nature.

———

HERE'S A SUMMARY OF THE KEY POINTS IN THIS CHAPTER:

- Once we see the inside-out nature of life, controlling ceases to make sense.
- The thoughts we have, create our feelings and so we always live in the feeling of our thinking.
- We live in a world of thought. Our mind works like a projector not a camera.
- We all have access to our own wisdom well
- True freedom has nothing to do with a clock or a business model.
- Insights come through mind shifts rather than mindset.

There's an 'insight' space below to journal any new thoughts that come through as you read:

———————————————————————

———————————————————————

———————————————————————

Next we'll talk about how to operate the advanced 'software,' we were born with.

3

OPERATING OUR HUMAN SOFTWARE

Being human is a bit like receiving the most advanced software as a gift at birth. Imagine trying to operate our software years after losing the instructions. We do okay, but gaining access to the operating manual is revolutionary.

It's a bit like the first time we ride a bicycle without stabilisers. We may look a bit shaky at first and might feel fearful of losing our balance as we wobble around on the seat trying something new. But when we begin to peddle and find our rhythm, we gather speed. Suddenly the wind's at our back and we gain momentum. Once we experience the thrill of effortless movement without stabilisers we don't want to bolt them to our wheels again.

Having an understanding of how our psychology works shows us we have the amazing capacity for true mental freedom. We don't need to be a psychologist to understand how our mind works. In fact, in some ways, the more we try to use our intellect to understand our experience of life, the more complicated it gets. We take our self further away from truth.

We'll look at how our Human Operating System really works, in a way which is simple to understand. It's unnecessary to drown in complicated psychological theory because fearless transformation doesn't happen through intellectual understanding. Personal insights or new ideas, pop into our mind when we're not even thinking about our problems. Have you noticed? The perfect solution arrives to the problem we've grappled with for months, as if out of the blue and with absolutely no overthinking.

This brings to mind, Einstein's, 'You can never solve a problem on the level on which it was created.'

When we glimpse how the system already works, we're able to begin to play the game of life and/or business with greater ease. We all have access to mental freedom. We always have. We just didn't know how it worked. Like all games, once we learn the rules, we gain confidence and enjoy playing. We have less on our minds about how we're performing, which naturally improves performance. This allows us to increase our odds in winning the game or at least in giving it our best shot.

THE WONDERFUL FEELING WE'RE ALL CHASING

When we have less on our mind we experience clarity and a wonderful feeling of being at peace with the world. This is what we all want on a deeper level even if we've never consciously thought about it this way. When we set big goals and decide to go after them, we're unconsciously chasing the wonderful feeling. We've all felt the delicious feeling of joy and contentment. Without a grounding in how the system works, we don't know where the feeling comes from and how to get it back. It's elusive and we can fall into the trap of chasing a feeling, which can feel frustrating.

As I shared in the previous chapter, we always experience the world from the inside-out. We often try to get back into the wonderful feeling through our circumstances. Sometimes we manage. Usually we don't. The feeling never comes from outside, but we experience it sometimes because it's an inbuilt feature of our human operating system.

Here are some common examples of when we try to find the wonderful feeling through goal setting:

- When we dream of being at the top of our field, we're chasing the wonderful feeling.
- When we decide to write a book and become a bestselling author, we're chasing the wonderful feeling.
- When we desire to own a big house, we're chasing the wonderful feeling.
- When we yearn to find our soul mate, we're chasing the wonderful feeling.
- When we set a goal to get fit, we're chasing the wonderful feeling.

And so it is with every goal ...

Goals can be wonderful but I'm sharing what I've seen about how to experience the wonderful feeling we're all chasing. We can experience it any time, with or without achieving a goal. I'm also pointing to how the system works so you can begin to see reliable principles already at work in every area of life. The reassuring thing about understanding how the system works is we don't need to learn anything new. Life already works this way. It works even when we're completely oblivious and we don't understand it. It works if we don't like the sound of it and wish we really lived in an 'outside-in' world.

IT'S LIKE GRAVITY

Gravity works all of the time even if we doubt it. The fact gravity exists is no longer called into question but there was a time when gravity was an unknown quantity. Sir Isaac Newton identified gravity around 1665. Legend has it that he was sipping tea at Trinity College, Cambridge, when he noticed an apple fall from a tree. There's still a 'Tree of Gravity' in the grounds of the college today. It's believed to be a descendent of the original tree which inspired Newton's insight about the forces of nature.

Gravity is a law of nature and so it's only important we believe in it in order not to endanger ourselves. It's helpful to know if we jump off a building, we'll hit the ground, unless Superman arrives to save us like he would Lois Lane. If gravity didn't work 100% of the time, navigating the world could prove quite tricky. For instance, a child, friend or pet might unexpectedly fly out of the window if we didn't tie them down. Everyday life would be even more unpredictable than it already seems.

One hot Summer's afternoon I was relaxing in the back garden in my favourite sun chair, sipping tea; like Newton might have done over 350 years ago. It had been a busy day and I felt the wonderful feeling of quiet contentment wash over me. In my experience, the wonderful feeling sometimes feels euphoric and at others it's a calm, gentle sense of wellbeing. It's a knowing everything is okay and we're connected to a deeper wisdom. It often feels as if we have all of the time in the world because there's nowhere to get to and nowhere else to be. The here and now is divine. This is the spiritual awakening Eckhart Tolle describes in 'The Power Of Now,' which years earlier I struggled to grasp. Now I see it was because I was trying to understand it intellectually. The wonderful feeling has a quality to it which is rich, quiet and deep and it's available to all of us all of the time.

I'd experienced a 'vertical leap' in my level of consciousness where I saw clearly for myself how life really works. This particular afternoon, I was in a meditative state and I noticed everything around me seemed bathed in technicolour. Recently I'd been stunned by the depth of vibrant colour as I walked our dog, Honey. I often stopped to stare in wonder and appreciate the beauty of the countryside. It seemed somehow more stunning than ever. How had I not noticed before?

I've read a lot of books in my quest to understand our spiritual and psychological experience. Once we're grounded in the principles of how life unfolds it's a lot simpler to understand than I thought. The books reveal a hidden depth of understanding so we're able to make sense of them and be impacted in very practical ways. What seemed like a beautiful description of spiritual enlightenment which I couldn't access, is available to all of us. It's a completely normal part of our human experience. This sudden flood of technicolour clarity reminded me of a scene in 'The Celestine Prophecy,' by James Redfield. I read the book and years later watched the film and was struck by the depth of colour people saw.

The Magic Mushroom

As I enjoyed the wonderful feeling, my eyes fell to a glowing, white mushroom on the flower bed which had popped up, fully formed, over night. 'This is the creative intelligence of the universe at work,' I thought, gazing at the mushroom in awe. I rose to take a closer look. It had surfaced from beneath the soil as a three inch mushroom in just a few hours, and seemed magical. And yet this amazing life force of creative intelligence works through us and is in everything around us, all of the time. We're made of creative intelligence. This is why there's nowhere to go to get it.

Meanwhile as I sat in my wondrous reverie, Honey had been sniffing around the mushroom and my wonder instantly turned to alarm as I suspected she may have nibbled it. I knew many wild mushrooms could be poisonous and in a split second my euphoric, meditative state shifted to panic. We'd lost our beloved cat a few years earlier to poison, and catastrophic thoughts flashed through my mind. If you've ever tried to search online for such things, you'll know it's not the best way to calm yourself. 'Is it this or that mushroom?' I questioned, clicking from image to image. With racing heart I looked at our sweet puppy and sent up a silent prayer she hadn't nibbled it. As much as the mushroom panic was a horrible experience, this serves as an illuminating example of how we live in our own virtual reality. At first I was immersed in the wonder of creation, and life had never looked more beautiful. Just a few seconds later, my 'projector' began streaming scary images onto my private movie screen about the deathly nature of poisonous mushrooms.

I doubt whether the mushroom was missing a piece, but

imagination is a powerful feature of our advanced human software. We can use the power of thought to create happy scenes or to freak ourselves out. I used my software in both ways in the space of about five minutes and our experience of reality can shift in a flash as mine did. Everything was exactly the same in the garden except my experience of reality. The euphoric lens switched to the panic lens in my virtual goggles. Only my thoughts changed. But for my sudden insecure thinking I could have continued to enjoy my meditative state which naturally occurred without a meditation ritual.

I feel it's important to be clear. This state of euphoria isn't one I experience every day. The wonderful feeling I'm pointing towards is available to us all when we allow our minds to settle. When we stop overthinking, we naturally fall into a peaceful state of mind. That day it felt particularly intense and euphoric but we all experience these shifts in our state of mind continuously even if we're unaware of them. This is how the mind works and so experiencing a low mood is normal too. There's no 'right' or 'better' state. My personal preference is euphoria but if I'm attached to the feeling, I suffer when I can't fall into it because the human experience is one of a natural ebb and flow.

It's normal to experience a gamut of emotions and when we see the truth of how it works, there's no need to try to fix our moods. They naturally shift on their own. Even better, when we give ourselves permission to enjoy our human experience; we live in a technicolour movie. Why limit our emotional range? We can appreciate the full range of emotions without self-judgement when we accept this is how we're designed. Now I'm free to feel not only love, joy, and euphoria but also feelings which are seen as negative, such as impatience, sadness or jealousy. When I feel the effects of thinking these kinds of 'negative' thoughts, I'm not as afraid of them as I used to be. I'm able to allow the thought storm to pass quickly. Thoughts are neutral. They are only ever coated with the toxic perception with which we tarnish them.

We are not our thinking and so we don't need to take our thinking seriously. This means our experience may range from a deep love for someone one minute, to feelings of irritation or anger the next. It doesn't give us important information about ourselves or the person we're thinking about. When we see it for our self, we're truly free to experience the natural highs and lows of relationships. Our moods are part of the ebb and flow of life. The impact this understanding has on the quality of all of our relationships, even with people who seem to get under our skin, is transformative.

The magic mushroom story is one of my personal experiences where I could easily spot the Three Principles of Mind, Consciousness and Thought in action. These principles explain how every human being experiences life, all of the time. There are no exceptions, just like there are no exceptions to the force of gravity. This is why Sydney Banks called them principles. He was an ordinary man, a 9th-grade educated welder who had an enlightenment experience. He saw, but for our insecure thinking in the moment, we always have mental wellbeing and clarity.

By gaining a deeper understanding of how these fundamental principles work, we deepen our grounding in how the human experience unfolds. It's far simpler than we tend to think but we've been indoctrinated to believe we live in an outside-in world. We're born with everything we need and instinctively know how to be content. As we grow, we fall into the same misunderstanding of reality which our teachers, parents and most of humanity live in.

WHAT ARE THE THREE PRINCIPLES?

MIND

There are many ways to describe the Principle of Mind. I imagine universal mind being like a computer which gives us access to the world wide web of all that has been and ever will be. Mind or Universal Mind is the energy of life which powers everything. One of the most beautiful benefits of Mind is when we begin to trust it has our back, we never feel completely alone again. We gain an awareness of it not being our job to manage the Universe or to attempt to control our experience.

Suddenly we see we have the whole power of the Universe at our fingertips and can tap into this infinite creative intelligence any time we like. It makes the job of life rest so much lighter on our shoulders. There's nothing for us to do to access this energy. 'Tapping into it' is simply a way to explain it. We're already sitting in creative intelligence. We're made of infinite potential and never know what amazing insight will pop into our mind at any second.

We've seen this in action throughout history with great creators such as Sir Isaac Newton and Albert Einstein. We see it in action flowing through Richard Branson, Oprah, JK Rowling and Elon Musk, to name a few extremely gifted creators. People with open minds enjoy the space for new ideas to flow in because they're connected to this limitless power supply. They receive insights which allow us to benefit from the inventions and solutions created by some of the most influential people in their fields.

There's another element to the Principle of Mind; called 'Personal Mind.' It's sometimes so called because Universal Mind has an impersonal flavour to it. Universal Mind can serve up an idea to many people at the same time. Whoever acts upon the insight first, may claim the idea, but really it popped into their head from the quantum computer of infinite potential.

I see 'Personal Mind,' as a bit like having restricted access to a computer with no working internet connection. Our personal mind is in a constant state of flux. One thought pops in, another floats out and this is how we experience reality through our personal mind. It's like having access to a hard drive which is full of old files, which we sift through, trying to find new data. There's no new data there, only facts or beliefs about what we already know. When we look to the unknown, we experience fresh insights and transformation with ease. Life changing ideas and solutions flow in from Universal Mind and we can only rest in this space when we're open to hanging out in the unknown.

CONSCIOUSNESS

Consciousness is one of the Three Principles and points to our level of consciousness or awareness of reality. We are all living at different levels of consciousness and our individual consciousness varies greatly from moment to moment. When my consciousness is low, my life looks hard. Situations seem like they will be difficult to handle. My energy feels low and it's as if I can't see clearly. I sometimes explain to my clients that when our consciousness is low, it reminds me of an eye which is a tiny slit open and we can't see much out of it. We have little, if any perspective because we can barely see what's in front of our nose. As our eye dilates, we have a much better view of reality. We have fresh perspective and can see opportunities and resources which are both under and beyond our nose. What looked like an impossible situation before, melts away and we can't even remember why we thought it was such a big problem.

The person who was driving us crazy yesterday when we looked at them through the slit of an eye, today seems perfectly reasonable or may even be transformed into an entirely different character. This is what consciousness does for us. Our whole view of life expands and we become effortlessly creative instead of insecurely reactive.

When our consciousness expands, nothing in our circumstances needs to change for everything to look and feel completely different. This is how we experience all of life. We just don't know it and so we fall for the illusion time and again. By being awake to this trick of the mind we're able to navigate our ups and downs more gracefully. When I feel down, I now know without a shadow of doubt I'll feel better soon. The old adage, 'This too shall pass,' points to the truth of the human condition.

THOUGHT

The Principle of Thought is what I pointed to when explaining the inside-out nature of life. Through thought we innocently create our version of reality. We have no control over the thoughts which pop into our mind but we can choose not to dwell on thoughts which create suffering for us. I spent years trying to be a positive thinker, not knowing I can't control the power of thought no matter how much I'd like to. Once we see we can't control which thoughts arrive in our mind; a bit like how we can't control which emails arrive in our inbox, we can choose not to engage with them.

If you're someone who puts a lot of stock into having a positive mental attitude, this awareness relieves a lot of self-created pressure because there's nothing to do at all to have one. When we stop trying to resist our thoughts, life becomes simpler. I was shocked when I discovered this truth but it freed up hours of my time previously spent in trying to fix my negative thinking.

We still have thoughts we'd rather not have, land in our mental inboxes but we don't need to fear them. It's a bit like smoking cigarettes knowing they pollute our lungs. We can stop smoking, just as we can end our habit of wallowing in our polluted thoughts. It may feel like we suffer from an addiction when we first recognise what's going on. The good news is our mind self-corrects beautifully without any intervention. In the same way we don't wake up in the morning and wonder how to talk, we don't need to worry about our thoughts either.

Sydney Banks said, "If the only thing that people learned was not to be afraid of their experience, that alone would change the world."

A DANGEROUS MISUNDERSTANDING OF REALITY

Just as I now see it was a waste of time trying to control my thinking for all of those years; it was also a misunderstanding of reality. This is how I view the understanding of the Three Principles as it becomes accessible across the world. It may seem revolutionary now to understand how our human operating system works in the way I'm describing.

Here's an example of how a misunderstanding of reality is later revealed as dangerous. In the future, it may seem as ridiculous to have believed in the old psychology and state-changing therapy techniques, as it does now to believe a lobotomy is a miracle cure for mental illness. This was the case in the 1940s and 1950s.

As we understand more about how our mind operates, we have access to more mental freedom, flow and clarity without any concentrated effort. To deepen our grounding in this revolutionary understanding of reality, there's nothing to do but there's always more to see. Let's continue looking in this direction together.

————

HERE'S A SUMMARY OF THE KEY POINTS IN THIS CHAPTER:

- We don't need to be a psychologist to have insight into how our psychology works.
- Fearless transformation doesn't happen through intellectual understanding which can instead take us further away from truth.
- The wonderful feeling is always available to us whether we set and achieve big goals or not.
- We are not our thinking and so we don't need to take our thinking seriously.

- The Three Principles Of Mind, Consciousness and Thought create our experience of life all of the time, whether we believe in them or not.

There's an 'insight' space below to journal any new thoughts that come through as you read:

_____

_____

_____

In the next chapter we'll look at why we are already fearless.

PART II

FEARLESS TRANSFORMATION

4

OUR INNATE FEARLESSNESS

Our wellbeing is innate and available to us at any given moment. It isn't determined by what happens 'out there,' as most people believe. This is why we are at our most resilient and resourceful when we kick into emergency mode. We've all heard stories where something awful happens and whole communities rise to the occasion and become fearless in the face of catastrophe.

I had many high drama experiences in my years living in Jerusalem. The one which really made an impression on me was during the Gulf War of 1990. I still remember hearing the wail of the sirens multiple times a day over a period of a couple of months. We were under daily threat of scud attacks from Saddam Hussein in Iraq. We never knew what or who would be hit next. You may think this sounds terrifying and wonder why I didn't return to Britain. Many of the visitors who didn't need to stay, left under warning from their embassy. My family begged me to return home but there was something compelling about being in the midst of chaos. I didn't want to abandon my friends. It felt easier to face the danger than to go back to Britain and worry from a distance. It was as if by staying, I could ensure my friends were okay. My gut instinct was to stay and so I did. I had a sense of confidence everything would be fine.

I was deeply touched by the goodwill and generosity people showed toward one another in this challenging time. It was something I hadn't experienced so intensely before. Perhaps the British 'Keep Calm And Carry On,' Second World War slogan evokes a feeling reminiscent of the camaraderie I felt in those special days. In accordance with precautions against chemical attack we sealed the bedroom with plastic sheeting. If I was at home when the siren sounded I would scoot into the room clutching the cat and the kettle. We never knew how long we'd be stuck in there. It could be anything from a few hours to all night so we had provisions ready. I stocked up on tins of food from the neighbourhood grocery store. I also hid a large, sharp knife in the dresser drawer. It gave me comfort when my imagination ran riot.

WE ARE NATURALLY RESILIENT AND CONFIDENT

We continued on with our lives in fearless spirit, gas masks with us wherever we went. I'd be waiting tables in the restaurant where I worked and when the siren sounded I'd pop my gas mask on until we got the all clear. I witnessed natural resilience in others and in myself which I might not have noticed if it weren't for being in this dangerous situation.

I don't remember being fearful. Now I can see more clearly why it was. When danger kicks in we are at our most resourceful and there's no time to spend worrying about what might happen. We're too engaged in the present moment. Humans are woken up to their infinite potential and are able to get out of their own way in the face of great adversity. What we usually don't see is we can do this any time. We don't need a catastrophe to occur in order to be resilient and effective.

In the early days of my transition from a job into having my own business I became a serious student of personal development. I learned to inoculate myself against negativity by avoiding watching the news. In my business circles it was frowned upon to watch television because it was considered a terrible waste of time. The message was, we should be building our business every spare minute of the day. These days I can watch the news, knowing my resilience can't be stolen by anyone. It's not dependent on the media's warped reporting. Even the BBC can't steal it, although sometimes I'm nearly caught out. It can't be taken away by a politician. I can be outraged when someone says something I don't agree with but I'm not in danger of being killed by negativity.

We do our own thinking. No one else has the power to do our thinking for us. No one can steal our peace of mind, even if it sometimes feels as though we're triggered by someone or something else. We never are. We don't need to protect ourselves once we know this. It's only ever our thinking about a situation which affects our state of mind. Others can't think for us; we do our own thinking.

We are all so much more resilient than we give ourselves credit for. I don't immerse myself in the bad news. When is there any good news on 'the news?' But it's wonderful to know in our bones we all have the capacity to be psychologically okay whatever happens. This is something we see more deeply through experiencing our own insights as we go deeper into this fearless understanding. And knowing people are okay doesn't mean we don't have compassion. I really feel for people more deeply than I ever have before because I'm now able to give myself permission to be human. I don't need to try to be constantly positive. It's normal for our moods to ebb and flow and when we think it isn't, we suffer. Suffering is optional.

I used to fear my sensitivity was a major flaw, especially after reading books like 'The Highly Sensitive Person.' I labelled myself a sensitive introvert. I've noticed many people seek to label themselves by taking personality tests. Whilst these tests can be useful in highlighting how we're currently showing up in the world, they're not at all helpful in revealing our true fearless nature. We each possess amazing, untapped potential. We limit our potential when we aim to package our self into a neat little box. In 'Living Fearlessly,' I seek to point upstream of our personality traits so we can uncover our true fearless nature which has no need to be labelled or categorised.

Fearlessness Transcends Ego

Our true fearless nature is a space within each of us which transcends ego. We know we're living from ego, which is the opposite of living fearlessly, when we feel insecure about how we're doing. We feel fearful of what others think of us. I've now given myself permission to accept my sensitivity as a healthy part of my nature. I no longer attempt to manage or control it. The problem with trying to control our state is, we can't become fearless by managing what we see as our flaws. Instead, we feel more isolated, fearful and different and have no idea we're operating from a very small, tight ego-filled space.

I'm not saying it feels good to be up against disaster, but knowing our resilience is always available, gives us a deep confidence. We can't access our innate confidence reliably through technique. This is because confidence comes from the inside and is already within us. It's an uncovering of our natural state so no forced state changing is required.

Working hard on myself has worked for me to a point, but it's a never ending battle. It fuels an internal struggle commonly known as resistance, especially in art and business. When we mistakenly believe external circumstances give us happiness, we think there are blocks we need to break through. We'll talk more about dissolving 'blocks' effortlessly with this fearless understanding, later in the book.

Given that confidence comes from the inside and is not something to be acquired, it's no wonder I was confused. I didn't understand why at times I was so confident and others felt so fearful. I didn't know how it worked. When people talk of someone being confident in their own skin this is what I think they mean. It's not some kind of artificial confidence we wear like an armour to protect our self. It's an integral part of our nature when we don't mess with it. Many people falsely believe their confidence comes from 'managing their state,'

We're all naturally confident, happy and fearless until we take ourselves away from peace of mind with insecure thinking in the moment. The more we get lost in our thinking, the more we're likely to suffer. This can be confusing in a society which respects and worships the intellect. It also explains why in the 21st century there are so many people complaining of feeling depressed or anxious. If external circumstances really created happiness, we'd be the happiest generation ever to walk the earth. In the western world we have more luxuries at our fingertips than ever before.

But no, the more we have, the more we seem to want. The more we want, the more we feel we lack. It used to bother me when people said, 'Money can't buy happiness.' I thought this was an attack on my personal philosophy. I judged the words as meme based and an effort to glamorise poverty, with its roots in religious teachings attempting to control people. Whilst I still believe this to be a part of some religious dogma, I've now seen it's impossible for money to make us happy anyway. I love the post adrenaline high of shopping or making a big sale as much as the next person but the happy feeling is short lived because it never came from the money in the first place.

The reason for this is because money doesn't possess the ability to make us happy. Money is neutral. It's only our habitual, fearful thinking about money which makes us feel worried. Our thoughts are transient as is the nature of happiness when dependent on how much money we have. Think about it; a nice big juicy sum of cash hits our bank account and we feel a rush of excitement. I like to do a little money dance. We're on a high, and feel confident we're on the right track. The following morning we're still a little exhilarated, but a couple of days later we wake up to find ourselves worrying again. 'Hold on a minute,' we think. 'What's going on? Why am I worrying when I made — insert whatever figure you want here — just the other day?'

And the figure could seem small or large. It doesn't matter either way because size is arbitrary. If we experience habitual thinking or toxic thought patterns where money is involved, they are going to repeat themselves no matter what the number. It's like having bugs in our software. I've noticed when I have 'a lot' of money, whatever it means to me, I become preoccupied about what I'm doing with it. When I decide I don't have 'enough' money I then fret about my perceived lack. There are probably few periods in-between where I don't worry about it all. I still have a lot to see on the topic of money. As a coach with certifications and training in money coaching, I've noticed this is a very common pattern with high achievers, and even those we consider wealthy. We misunderstand that money is neutral, the same as everything else we seek to acquire to feel better. There's no amount of money capable of giving us the permanent peace of mind we crave.

MY BANK ACCOUNT WAS A SOCK

Recently I was thinking back to the time when my bank account was a sock. It's funny to think about it now, given that these days I think my bank accounts are so important. I'd forgotten how I used to work three jobs in Jerusalem and used to stash my cash in a black and purple sock in the bedroom drawer. I didn't think it strange at the time. This is an example of how when we don't have a lot of insecure thinking about a situation, it's as if it doesn't exist. If I'd been caught up about needing to have a bank account, I would probably have felt unhappy. I wasn't officially permitted to work in Jerusalem all of those years ago but I worked anyway. I didn't earn a great deal of money but I seemed to have a pretty good life all the same. And I had no savings other than whatever I managed to keep in the sock, beyond what was needed for rent, food and other basics.

Now, I'm not saying having a bank account doesn't make financial logistics easier, especially in this digital world we live in. However, there was a beautiful simplicity to my life back then which I didn't appreciate at the time. If I had the ability to be happy when my entire financial plan was in a sock, it puts my finances into perspective. Now when I fret about what's going on with my bank account, I can come to it from a lighter place. Most of the time I can glimpse beyond my personal, insecure thinking. I see that the number fluctuates as much as my state of mind and the two are not intimately connected.

I want to be clear about this. I'm not independently wealthy and I do need to work to pay for what I want. So if you're thinking, 'Oh, it's okay for her. If I had enough money in my bank account I'd also be able to come to it lightly,' then this is a great example of how we live in the feeling of our personal thinking. I've been, shall we say, low on funds, many times in my life and wasn't born rich. I've experienced the feelings of fear we can create for ourselves when we think our wellbeing comes from money. I grappled with this a lot in conversations with my mentors. I said things like, 'Surely I'm better off with more money. What if I can't feed my kids? That would be really bad, wouldn't it?' I thought they meant I need to be happy with no money. It wasn't until I had a big personal insight, I saw what they meant, not what I thought they meant.

The point is not that we must feel joy at the idea of having no money. It's more about knowing we'll always be okay. If and when we're in a situation such as not having the money we need, no matter how terrible it seems, our inner wisdom or intuition will still be available to us. We'll find a way but we won't know what the way is until we're in the situation. This is why it's a waste of energy to try to anticipate the future because we have no idea what will happen. This is how it always works in every area of our lives but money seems to evoke deep fear in many of us. When we get lost in doom and gloom thinking, our clarity is impaired. This in turn makes it harder to create the money we desire.

Money doesn't solve all of our problems. In fact, money doesn't even solve our money problems. When we fail to grasp this basic concept we make decisions about our money problems from a place of insecurity. Insecure thinking inspires reactive rather than resourceful behaviour and so usually doesn't result in good money decisions. When we see the truth about where our experience comes from, we also gain the clarity to see what, if anything, needs to be done about our perceived money problem.

Often these problems disappear all on their own because they were created by looking at them from a certain perspective or level of consciousness. I'm sure you've heard people say, 'I have no money.' It's rarely true; it's simply their low consciousness in the moment leading them to feel as though they have 'no money.' Our thoughts create our feelings all of the time so if we feel like we have no money, we're thinking, 'no money' thoughts. When we have less respect for our thoughts, we let them pass through our minds with ease.

THE IMAGINARY PROBLEM

Once we are clear on the imaginary problem which is our fearful thinking about what money means to us, we're open to receive new resourceful ideas. We have more access to new ideas to help us to make more money, or manage what we have without angst.

A new idea could be anything from:

'Stop spending so much on stuff I don't need in an effort to make myself feel better,' to

'I think I'll create something new to make a new stream of income,' or

'I have no idea what to do now so I won't take any action until I get some clarity.'

And the beauty of it is there's nothing to do to fix our thinking. We only need to recognise it for the illusion it is and let our thoughts pass by. New thoughts are like buses; there's always another one along in a minute.

Money isn't the number one fear for everyone but I chose it as an example because it is for so many of us. In business we usually have more situations where we need to either ask for money or pay money to run our enterprises. Whether in business or not, the odds are we have at least one situation which repeatedly finds us spinning in insecure, fearful thinking. It might be our relationship, parenting, weight, business, money or any number of things. Life becomes easier and more enjoyable, even by glimpsing that our insecure thinking doesn't represent the tangible problem we thought. Just because we feel horrible today, doesn't mean we'll feel horrible tomorrow, or even in an hour's time. When we stop taking our moods seriously they're less of a serious condition. In fact they fix themselves without any intervention from us whatsoever.

If fearless is our natural state why are we so often in a state of turmoil and unhappiness? The clue is in the 'state.' Our state of mind reflects our thinking at any given time. Our thoughts create our feelings and when we begin to notice we're feeling insecure or fearful, it's a good indication our thinking has gone offline. It's as if we lose our connection and need a reboot. It's a bit like when our phone stops working and we turn it off. As if by magic, perfect working order is resumed instantly when we turn it back on.

Because we don't understand how our minds work, we argue for our contaminated thinking. We think it's giving us real data about our 'problem.' We innocently don't see our only problem is our thinking. It reminds me of what I call the sour milk analogy. The taste of sour milk is disgusting. We don't need to make an empowered decision to avoid drinking it. We taste sour milk and naturally have no desire to repeat the experience. We discard the milk without a second thought. Instead of discarding our contaminated thinking like sour milk, we take it seriously.

We've been indoctrinated to believe there is a benefit to wallowing in our psychology in the mistaken belief we can fix our problems by thinking about them. The more we see the value of not trying to get in there and tamper with what's in our head, our minds quietly settle because that's how the mind is designed. Instead of arguing for our current version of reality why not allow ourselves to be content? No one needs fixing. We're not broken whatever we may have been telling our self until now. We all have the capacity for new, fresh thought at any moment. Fresh thought leads to effortless transformation.

LIVING FEARLESSLY AT ANY AGE

I've noticed lately how many people talk about their lives as if it's too late to do what they really want. As if because they didn't do what they think they should have done years ago, it's no longer an option. Perhaps they feel they failed to achieve what they were really attached to having. Or they judge themselves harshly for making the wrong decision 'when they were younger.'

This is sad for many reasons but here are two that come to mind:

1) Many people are lost in thought wishing they'd done whatever they wanted to do, better or differently, in their twenties, thirties or forties. Upon reflection they think they could have done it then but now they're older, they decide they're definitely 'too old.'

2) Another bunch of people in their fifties, sixties, seventies or even eighties or nineties are doing what they fancy, when they fancy it. They no longer judge themselves harshly about what they should have done. They're too busy doing what they can do to regret what they didn't do. They would love to be back in their younger years now they've understood how much fun life is when we stop worrying what other people think.

Which group is happiest? What strikes me as really crazy is many of the people in example one have wonderful lives and are often seen as extremely successful. The problem is, they're so busy wishing they'd done something differently, they miss the beauty of the life they're living right now.

Do we make mistakes? Absolutely. But what's the point dwelling on the past? We did what we did and because of some of what we did, we are where we are today. Life is short. For some it's really short, as I was reminded when my brother died of a heart attack at age 48. So many of us watch our lives pass us by with a feeling of quiet desperation. We're terrified of upsetting the status quo and being judged. We're fearful and so we don't make the changes we would love to make.

WE DON'T HAVE TO TAKE OURSELVES SO SERIOUSLY! (REALLY)

Even though we've been led to believe that getting serious is what it takes to achieve our dreams, I've fallen in love with a lighter, simpler way of living. This is what inspired me to write this book. What if we didn't have to make everything so hard and take everything quite so seriously?

How many of us are doing beautifully until someone informs us it's time to get serious? The stakes are high. 'You'd better bring your A Game.' Control freak, Type A Personality, super competitive, high achieving, go-getter types are susceptible to taking themselves out of the game when things go wrong. I know a lot of people like this. Many of my favourite people in my network are this way. Birds of a feather flock together, it seems. The great news is it doesn't have to be this way. There is a lighter experience of life available which doesn't require striving, suffering, pushing, perfecting and making things happen.

When we unhook our self from our regrets and the common 'am I good enough?' thinking, we can take the first or next step to create what we want. And if we stumble and fall, so what? We may think everyone's watching and judging us but really, most people are lost in their own heads, worrying about their own insecurities. They have little time to notice when we stumble. This is a sobering truth but one which allows us to give ourselves permission to live fearlessly.

Our self-worth doesn't depend on us getting it right. We're free to play with our potential. And it turns out that playing is one of the most useful 'success techniques' out there. People don't talk about it much because they're usually seeking the secret information they've been told they must have to be successful. What if playing around, giving it a try and making a mistake, or not, didn't mean anything about our value as a human being? Those with Type A tendencies may find this really uncomfortable to even contemplate.

When we take our self too seriously it can destroy any hopes of the project we're working on coming to life. But if we instead enjoy creative playtime and see our work as a game, we can carry on with the next step. Ego would have us think, to be successful we need to be really serious. As I see more about how the game of life works, this looks less and less useful to me. If 'being serious' helps us to create what we want, then great. For most it's much more of a hindrance than a help.

Even the idea of being serious is an illusion. It's another label we've saddled our self with. When being serious loses its appeal and we start to doubt our 'self,' we can push the reset button which allows us to go back to playing the game. In the game we're always fearless because it's simply a game. And this is where we find the freedom to play full out and fearless because we're less attached to the outcome. We can still do things we think are 'serious' such as our life's work, or not. Our self-worth is a thought created construct which fluctuates with our thoughts. It does not depend on what we do or don't do. It's enough to be alive.

In the big roulette 'wheel' of life, anything is possible when we live fearlessly. When we open our eyes, the evidence is all around us. How about Vera Wang who began her career as a designer at age 40? Now she's one of the premier designers in the world. Or consider Charles Darwin who wasn't well known before he wrote, 'On The Origin Of Species,' at age 50 and had a dramatic impact on the scientific community with his theory of evolution. Then there's Ray Kroc who was a salesman before buying MacDonald's at age 54. And finally; how about Anna Moses known as 'Grandma Moses' who began her painting career at age 78? One of her paintings later sold for $1.2 million. It's never too late to begin living fearlessly. We are free to make choices to do what we love.

———

HERE'S A SUMMARY OF THE KEY POINTS IN THIS CHAPTER:

- We don't need a catastrophe to occur in order to be resilient and effective.
- It's normal for our moods to ebb and flow and when we think it isn't, we suffer. Suffering is optional.
- Our true fearless nature is a space within us which transcends ego.
- We're all naturally resilient, confident and fearless until we take ourselves away from peace of mind with insecure thinking in the moment.

- Money is neutral. It's only our thoughts about money which make us feel happy or worried.
- No one needs fixing. We're not broken whatever we may have been telling our self until now.
- We all have the capacity for new, fresh thought at any moment.
- We don't have to take our self so seriously! (Really)

There's an 'insight' space below to journal any new thoughts that come through as you read:

_____

_____

_____

Next we'll look at dissolving fear effortlessly without working on our self.

5

DISSOLVING FEAR EFFORTLESSLY

Dissolving fear doesn't require us to become fearless warriors. Blocks have been given an almost mythical power in the world of personal growth literature. We're challenged to go into battle to conquer resistance in a warlike fashion. This is a very masculine, ego based approach. I believe it's out of balance with the feminine energy needed to raise the consciousness of our planet. We construct this made up reality though our personal thinking.

OUR MISGUIDED BELIEFS ABOUT BLOCKS

We experience our own habitual thought patterns through our personal thinking in the same way we experience our separate realities. It's popular to label the thought patterns we don't like, 'resistance' or 'blocks.' It seems as though everywhere I look there are magic bullets promising to give us a quick fix so we can be happy once we get rid of our 'block'. The so-called block means we have a thought or some thoughts on our mind which trouble us when we think them. They don't trouble us when we don't think them. We can choose not to dwell on a situation which repeatedly troubles us, and we'll see this is always true. It demonstrates that whatever troubles us isn't permanent. Our perspective continuously shifts with our thoughts. Don't take my word for it. Pay attention and you'll notice how it works.

Traditional approaches from therapy to NLP to life-coaching and all kinds of methodologies in-between, focus on finding efficient ways to deal with blocks. How brilliant would it be to not have to do anything about them at all? We've been indoctrinated to believe there's 'no pain, no gain.' We roll up our sleeves and 'do the work.' This is author, Stephen Pressfield's battle cry in his best-selling books about creativity and resistance. I'm not saying we shouldn't work, but it's a different kind of work to what we may think. What if we didn't have to make such heavy weather of 'the work' in order to achieve what we want? What if all we have to do is show up in the moment and be fully present to whatever shows up?

There are thousands of online courses about how to clear various types of blocks, and the self-help sections at the book stores are crammed full. I've invested many thousands of pounds over the years in systems, courses, coaches and books to help me clear whatever blocks I felt I suffered from. Fortunately, as we experience our own insights about the nature of thought, we see that battling to clear our thoughts is counter-productive. The mind has a self-clearing function which requires absolutely no effort from us at all. Our minds reset to their default setting of clarity when we don't jump in there and try to fix them.

'Almost everything will work again if you unplug it for a few minutes, including you.' Anne Lamott

It's a bit like having computer trouble. Once we calm down enough to see the wisdom in not bashing our computer keys, we can switch off our device. It turns out our computer simply got confused because we had multiple windows open simultaneously. Now if we didn't know how the system works, we might make up frightening scenarios and lie awake half of the night worrying about needing to buy a new computer.

If normal service isn't resumed when we reboot our computer, it quickly becomes obvious it needs repairing. This is the same in all areas of life; sometimes there's action to take but very often there isn't. We have a tendency to get lost in our future fearful thinking and create a lot of problems which don't exist. We tend to think there are benefits to fearful thinking because it means we're prepared and alert for every potential disaster. If this was how life worked then it would make perfect sense. But it never works this way. The scenarios we would most like to be prepared for, usually hit like a tornado we could never anticipate.

What if resistance truly isn't real? What if blocks are pure illusion? If it were true, what would we do about our blocks? We don't need to take any action to blast through made up blocks even though they feel so real. When we don't know this, we decide to try to make whatever we want to happen through sheer force of will. We tell ourselves:

- We'll write the book if it kills us ...
- We'll build the business even if we die trying

- We'll get down to our clothes size from ten years ago even if we have to starve.
- We'll buy the latest meditation system and plonk our bottom down on the cushion even if we've got a 'monkey mind' as the Buddhist's call it, and our toes twitch!

I used to feel restless when I forced myself to meditate because I thought I needed to do something to have a quiet mind. No matter what system or manifestation technique we practice, it is normal for our minds to wander. We may find our self wondering 'Why is it so difficult to create what I want?' or 'What's wrong with me?' 'All of those successful people seem to make it look so easy.'

A GLIMPSE OF THE TRUTH

As we look in this direction, our busy mind begins to slow down and we glimpse the truth. When we see for our self that blocks are pure figments of our imagination, we realise there's absolutely nothing to do to clear them. They are 100% made of thought. It's as pointless as trying to catch clouds, one at a time, so we can see the sky. We could spend all day trying to clear the clouds but wouldn't it be a better use of our time to wait until they drift by of their own accord? Imagine how frustrated we would be trying to catch clouds. Even if we devised a miracle step-by-step system to clear the clouds, they'd probably be back clogging up the sky the next day.

And then we might start beating our self up because we're not worthy of a clear sky. Other more worthy people can enjoy the blue sky but we have blocks so must suffer until breaking through with a cloud clearing system.

And on it whirls in our frantic, busy mind. This may seem like an exaggerated example but it's fruitless to spend so much time focusing on what we think is wrong with us. It's all made of transient thought anyway. Instead of spending our precious time working on blocks, or in my case journalling thousands of pages in hundreds of notebooks over the past thirty years, we could simply get on with life. When our mind clears we see that anything is possible. There's nothing to do but to see the possibility.

WHEN WE UNDERSTAND THIS WE ARE FREE TO:

- Have a go at writing the book
- Launch the new project
- Take the day off, without worrying
- Show up and respond to what shows up
- Lose the weight and shape up
- Start a new business
- Go on a date with someone 'out of my league.'
- End a relationship
- Marvel at the beauty of the sky as the clouds drift by
- Play with our kids even if we didn't make as much money as we wanted

HOW LIFE REALLY WORKS

And the list goes on ... This may seem simple and in some ways it feels like we've known it forever. This is how the system works but we lose sight of it. We knew this when we were kids but somewhere along the way we learned to over-complicate and overthink our every move. Why continue to spend so many days of our life cloud clearing? Once we see we are the sky not the clouds, the weather is of little consequence to our mood.

EVEN ANXIETY IS JUST THOUGHT

As I shared earlier, I struggled with anxiety since I was sixteen. I tried many different therapies and approaches to get rid of what I viewed as a serious block to my happiness. Anyone who's suffered from the symptoms of anxiety knows how debilitating the experience can feel. It's as if your body isn't in your control. People respond to their stressful thoughts in different ways. In my case anxiety manifested as panic attacks and an underlying fear of being visible, which impacted many areas of my life. By the age of twenty-two I had just about learned to manage my anxiety. It no longer dictated everything I did or didn't do but I was far from free of it. Fear continued to linger below the surface which made my world feel small. Anxious people limit their lives by only allowing themselves to do things they believe they can control.

The fear of being visible is very common and comes up a lot in my coaching sessions with clients. Many people, especially women, are petrified of being judged and don't give themselves permission to have fun playing the game of business and life. As a young woman I knew I wasn't shy. I could initiate a conversation with anyone and was often very outgoing so I could see clearly this wasn't the cause of my anxiety. Even when we see our self as shy, we're not really, we just think we are. We can ditch any personality construct once we see the deeper truth of how we create them.

Anxiety and fears manifest in our behaviour. They may show up as eating disorders, self-harming, addictions to toxic substances, social avoidance, fear of public speaking, fear of flying, agoraphobia, relationship drama, needing to prove oneself, or numerous other phobias.

Emotionally or psychologically, fears and anxiety often show up as feelings of unworthiness, depression, guilt, sadness, self-doubt, procrastination, perfectionism, overwhelm and/or fear of failure. Physiological symptoms could be anything from panic attacks, excessive sweating, nervous rashes, nausea, blushing, palpitations, pins and needles, headaches and shortness of breath, to name the most common.

There is no end to the number of problems we can create for ourselves when we don't understand what's going on 'under the hood' of our minds. We use the infinite creative potential of the universe against our greater good and it's popular to call it self-sabotage.

Anxious people feel as though their world is spinning out of control and they're a victim of circumstance. They think if they can control their panic attacks, their body, their feelings and/or their thoughts, they'll be okay. And in a way it's true. Anxiety manifests because of the misunderstanding of how our experience of life works. We all feel anxious or fearful sometimes, even if we've not labelled ourselves as officially having 'anxiety.' It's a normal part of being human to feel on edge sometimes. When we believe our thoughts are real, i.e., I'm not good enough, I'm too fat, I'm not pretty enough, I'm not clever enough, I'm not talented enough, I'll never be successful, I don't believe in myself, I'm too old, etc., it seems sensible to try to control them.

In my younger years, I knew nothing about this new understanding, but I experienced an insight prior to my anxiety breakthrough. I saw early on, I was manufacturing my own anxiety through anxious thinking. The problem was, I didn't know how to stop it. I also believed my thoughts were true. My 'software' frequently ran on high-alert mode which felt exhausting.

I don't think most people who knew me back then would say I was anxious. They might say I was a good laugh. Those who worked with me would probably say I was professional and good at my job. And I was. I was placing foreign currency deals for large sums of money at the age of seventeen. When I returned from my travels at the age of twenty-two it wasn't long before I was promoted into a leadership role at a large investment bank. No matter how firmly we pigeon hole ourselves with some kind of failing or disorder, sometimes our true nature shines through. It's how it works. People become very good at hiding anxiety, stress and fear because they're ashamed they experience them. This then fuels anxious thinking and becomes a vicious cycle of self-hatred, guilt and shame.

People who suffer from some type of fear, phobia or 'block,' often learn to manage their symptoms well enough for others to not notice. It doesn't mean they're not suffering inside. I wish I'd known I wasn't the only one. There's a tendency to label ourselves as a special case. We think no one else struggles in the way we do. This isn't at all helpful and only makes us feel more isolated. It's also a lie. There's no right way to manage our fears but there's tremendous hope when we know fear can dissolve effortlessly. We don't need to spend years trying to break through mythical blocks. The more focus and attention we give something, the more it seems to demand.

I'm not fond of sharing my story of anxiety because I still find it a bit embarrassing. I'm sharing my experience because I know others suffer from similar fears. I also realised anxiety is no different at its root than any other kind of 'block.' All blocks or patterns can be dissolved through our personal insights. This is the only way our habitual thinking ever permanently disappears. After realising I was unknowingly creating my own anxiety I saved hundreds of pounds for a course of hypnotherapy. I remember being so ashamed someone might see me going into the office. Anxiety and any type of mental illness still seem to bear quite a stigma but when I was a young girl I don't remember ever hearing anyone even talk about anxiety. I didn't really know it was a valid 'thing.' I just knew I felt bad a lot of the time. Now we hear it spoken of often, but people still don't understand that the more we try to fix it, the more it shows up.

It may sound as though hypnotherapy enabled me to manage my anxiety. What happened was I had an insight about how I think, and how I didn't need to think that way. The hypnotherapy was helpful to me in as much as I finally spoke about what was on my mind. As my thoughts slowed down, there was space for some fresh thinking. It no longer felt like such a shameful deep, dark secret. I didn't tell anybody what I was doing except for my best friend as I didn't want to worry my family. I thought they wouldn't understand.

When I was introduced to this new understanding I hadn't

suffered from panic attacks for years. I was no longer fearful of speaking in public or being visible, but I still seemed to have what's sometimes called 'low-grade anxiety.' It was a feeling of not always being safe. I used to try and control my circumstances when I felt fearful so I'd never feel anxious. I thought feeling fearful and anxious was a defect in me and something I needed to work on. And so over the years I worked and worked on myself.

Through this understanding, I began to see more about the nature of our true fearless selves and I saw, not only were my thoughts made up but my whole idea of 'myself' was made up. I read about this in spiritual literature but never really understood it. We can read books and intellectually understand what's being said but it's not until we have our own insights that our experience of 'our self' completely shifts.

These wise words by spiritual masters point to what I mean by our true fearless self:

'The ego is only an illusion, but a very influential one. Letting the ego-illusion become your identity can prevent you from knowing your true self. Ego, the false idea of believing that you are what you have or what you do, is a backwards way of assessing and living life."

— WAYNE DYER

'True self is non-self, the awareness that the self is made only of non-self elements. There's no separation between self and other, and everything is interconnected. Once you are aware of that you are no longer caught in the idea that you are a separate entity."

— THICH NHAT HANH

We are not our insecurities and we're not even our talents, as much as we'd like to think we are. Our experience of who we are is created from thought, just as our experience of everyone else is fashioned through thought. That's why we adore some people whilst others don't seem able to bear them. They've created a different version to the one we created! We see more of the good in someone we love than another who doesn't care for them. And this applies to us too. We can create a wonderful version or a not good enough version of ourselves.

The 'not good enough' pattern of thinking is prevalent in many people's experience in different scenarios. We may feel extremely competent in most areas but not good enough in another. Or it could be the other way around. We feel competent in one area but lacking in others. When feeling low we might feel unworthy across all areas.

All it takes for this to change is a new thought. The 'not good enough' thoughts and feelings of unworthiness are simply part of a habitual thought pattern. A habitual thought pattern occurs when we have one thought, or a small army of thoughts we tend to think a lot. We think them so often we believe they must be true. It's a bit like the famous saying sometimes attributed to Nazi Germany's, Propaganda Minister, Goebbels.

'If you repeat a lie often enough, people will believe it, and you will even come to believe it yourself.'

This is known in psychology as 'the illusory truth effect,' and seems to work extremely well in convincing people of the veracity of something. It's no wonder we believe our thoughts when we don't understand how the mind works. We are literally getting in there 'under the hood' and brainwashing ourselves. We know no better.

I Saw Something New About An Old Problem

More recently, my anxiety dramatically reduced in all areas but I still felt, 'morning dread.' I experienced this most days since the age of sixteen. I'd wake up in the morning and feel like I was being attacked by a flood of anxious thoughts. I was already a lot better at dealing with it and would get up, make some tea and begin my day. Gradually the anxious thoughts would subside and I would start to feel like myself again. When I was sixteen I had no idea my thoughts weren't real and it felt terrifying.

I was in a coach training with my wonderful friend Kim Kasse. Our mission was to coach each other on a topic we wanted an insight around and so I brought my 'morning dread.' By this time I'd resigned myself to never being completely anxiety-free because no matter how much I understood, I couldn't seem to see anything new.

There's no value in indulging these thoughts but I still had a deep desire to not think them at all. You may be able to relate. I wanted to be rid of them! I learned we're not in control of our thoughts as I once believed so it was clear there was no point trying to vanquish them. But what else could I do? I was at a loss and felt frustrated.

My expectations were high because I'd heard so many stories of people having complete turnarounds through the understanding of these principles. There are cases of people diagnosed with mental illness who after being exposed to the principles, experience a complete recovery. People see for themselves that nothing can permanently damage who they are. Principles practitioners and coaches are sharing this new understanding around the world, in organisations, ranging from corporate companies to prisons and everything in-between. The results are incredible. How come my morning dread wouldn't shift?

I regaled Kim with my sad story and I don't remember any of our conversation except for one line. Kim said, 'What if you have thoughts in the morning that aren't like big barges but are more like little boats?'

IT'S ONLY A BUSY MIND!

And I heard something in those words about my experience being just another form of a 'busy mind.' I'd already seen that having a busy mind gets in the way of clarity but I hadn't even considered my anxiety could be as simple as experiencing a busy mind. As we left for the day, I still doubted this would make any difference to my so called, 'morning dread.'

That night in my rented cottage in Venice Beach I fell into a beautiful, deep sleep. At about 5am I awoke and felt the most wonderful feeling of peace and clarity. I remember wondering what life would be like if more people knew this feeling more of the time. Have you ever felt a feeling of absolute joy and peace at being alive? The more we immerse ourselves in this understanding the more we see. There's no guarantee of when we'll have a big 'AHA.' We experience our own unique insights in the form of new thoughts which pop into our mind. This is how the system works but when we don't know what to look for, we often miss the significance.

As with all insights, mine may not mean much to you. There's something about the nature of our own insights which shifts or expands our consciousness. Even when nothing has changed in our external world, we are different. We show up differently. We create people differently. This is why I'd rather help people to change in a way which facilitates permanent transformation.

If you're wondering what the significance of the boats and barges was for me, here's what I mean. I already understood my experience was aggravated by the fear of the fearful thinking or anxiety, but I still dreaded the thoughts bombarding me in the mornings. I suddenly saw through this transformative coaching conversation, when my thoughts come thick and fast, it's still only a 'busy mind.' This is a term we use in this work to describe being lost in insecure, fast-paced thought. This is why the term 'lost in thought,' is so common. For some reason until then, I'd categorised my anxious thoughts as different from others. It was a great relief to see they are no more special than any of the thoughts which trickle into my mind. I'd innocently labelled them as dreadful.

Since then I've had a different relationship with morning dread. The vision of the barges shifted something fundamental in my thinking. Early that morning I experienced an absolute knowing that my wellbeing is always intact. It's not a prescription and I could talk about barges all day long and another person might see nothing. The only prescription there is for transformation if there is one, is the more we look for universal truth, the more we see it. What we see is perfect for our own personal transformation.

When I coach from these fearless principles, we look to the new and unknown. We don't look towards stale how-to formulas and techniques which may or may not have worked for others. A great Transformation Coach who has grounding in this understanding can see a client's blindspots. Clients sometimes say, 'Oh, so that's just thought too!' As we gain new awareness, we see what was previously invisible to us. It's a bit like peeling an onion. Every layer we remove, reveals a perfect, shiny new layer underneath. There's always more to uncover about what we don't yet see. We're like fish in water. We don't see the water because we're immersed in it.

I work with my clients to unleash their fearless true nature. As we see more about the creative potential of the universe and how we are made of infinite possibility, a lot of impossibles simply drop away without concentrated effort.

And I'll end this chapter with a quote from Marcus Aurelius.

'People look for retreats for themselves, in the country, by the coast, or in the hills . . . There is nowhere that a person can find a more peaceful and trouble-free retreat than in his own mind. So constantly give yourself this retreat, and renew yourself.'

HERE'S A SUMMARY OF THE KEY POINTS IN THIS CHAPTER:

- The 'blocks' which trouble us aren't permanent because our perspective constantly shifts with our thoughts.
- Working to clear our blocks is as pointless as trying to

catch clouds. Allowing them to drift on of their own accord is a better use of our time.

- Even anxiety is just a busy mind. There's nothing for us to do except to understand more about how our mind works.
- There's no guarantee of when we'll have a big 'AHA,' We experience our own unique insights in the form of new thoughts which pop into our mind.
- For transformation we look to the new and unknown, not to stale how-to formulas and techniques which may or may not have worked for others.

There's an 'insight' space for you below to journal any new thoughts that come through as you read:

_____

_____

_____

Next we'll look at how we are the leader of our own life.

6

___

BECOMING THE FEARLESS LEADER OF
OUR LIFE

'As soon as you trust yourself, you will know how to live.'

— GOETHE

How many things do you do because you care what other people think?

If the answer to the question is, 'none,' perhaps you believe you're the empowered leader of your life. However, it may be ego running the show. It's wise to wake up to our ego or fearful little self. Often it plays tricks on us.

If this is the case then we're being guided by insecurity rather than intuition. What if we really saw that our freedom lies in operating beyond judgement of our self and the judgement of others? What if our insecure thoughts, the content of which is no more relevant than the insecure way we choose to react to them, weren't a factor in the choices we make? Freedom is a state of mind, not a destination.

The common personal development question, 'What would you do if you knew you couldn't fail?' is only helpful in uncovering what we're inspired to do in a 'perfect world.' In the real world we have no way of knowing whether we'll 'fail' or succeed. In fact, failure is also made of thought and depends entirely on what we've decided constitutes failure. One person's failure is another person's success. It's all relative to how we judge our results.

FAILURE ISN'T FATAL

Results are results even if they're not the ones we want. Failure, whatever it looks like to each of us, is a sign we've given something a shot. I no longer have any desire to try to motivate myself or others. Living fearlessly goes far beyond a temporary external boost of motivation to pump someone up. Failure really can't touch us unless we believe our self-worth is at stake. If we think our self-worth will be delivered to us via our latest success, we're operating from ego and insecurity. Sometimes we get what we want and sometimes we don't. This is the perfect world we live in. Imagine how crazy life would be if we instantly got everything we thought we wanted?

Who knows what kind of chaos we'd unwittingly create. There's a grander plan unfolding and we don't know what it is yet. If we achieve everything we desired on a whim we'd probably lose our sense of appreciation and achievement for when life goes our way.

The beauty of seeing this for our self is our insecurity begins to dissolve. We can be vulnerable and even when we fear looking stupid, it matters less. We might be embarrassed for a moment.

The looking stupid may not be apparent to the other person we're so concerned about anyway. We manufacture endless insecurity when we wear our 'I'm not worthy,' goggles. It's counterintuitive because we think we're being humble, but really we're trapped in the ego of our small, fearful self. In this space we can never win. Ego will always outsmart us. We'll always need a faster car, a higher profit, a more charming husband, a sexier wife, a slimmer body, a firmer six-pack or whatever it may be. It's an exhausting game because we set our self up to lose no matter how well we play.

Fear of failure, fear of being judged and fear of looking stupid stop us from trusting our intuition and being the fearless leader of our life. We protect our self by playing safe. I'm not saying not to be mindful of how our actions affect others. But most of the time they don't have as big an impact as we fear. The judgement is what we're scared of; what people think scares the hell out of us.

These words of wisdom from Winston Churchill illustrate this beautifully:

> 'Success is not final, failure is not fatal: it is the courage to continue that counts.'

People are more resilient than we give them credit for. Our ego tries to fool us into believing their wellbeing depends on us. It doesn't. As part of my living fearlessly exploration, I've been doing an experiment to see how vulnerable I can be. I've spent a lifetime trying to protect myself from potential pain. Believing what happens in our world is all about us, only adds to our suffering.

The truth is that people do what they do and often don't even take us into account. They're following their own intuition or insecurity. If the fall-out of what they do hits us hard it's our default system to make it all about us. 'How can they do this to me?' Or, 'Am I not good enough?'

In relationships, making the situation all about us is like rubbing salt into the wound and splashing it with vinegar to make sure the wound really stings. Later, on reflection, we're usually able to see what unfolded was much better for us in the long run. Now we have the perspective to see if we hadn't been fired from the job, which was such an assault to our ego at the time, we wouldn't have moved to a new city and found a more fulfilling career. If our marriage hadn't ended we wouldn't be with our soulmate. If our business hadn't failed we wouldn't have started a new business which revealed a completely different path. We try to hack a path through the jungle, not seeing there's already a path unfolding effortlessly with each step we take. The path is easier to navigate when we're awake to how life really works. Hacking isn't required when there's no jungle.

We think we can predict our future based on our past but we can't. It doesn't work this way. We don't know what's on the cards for us so there's no point trying to jump in and micro-manage every situation. It only leads to frustration when the deck doesn't instantly give us the hand we crave.

TRANSFORMATION COACHING QUESTIONS

- Looking back, can you connect up the dots in your own life of one event leading to another which could never have happened but for what seemed like disaster at the time?

- What if you could let go of your constant need to be liked, loved, and respected?
- What if you begin to trust yourself to make decisions from what feels right to you, not from your knee-jerk reactions to circumstances?
- What might transform in your life if you get out of your own way and allow whatever wants to happen to unfold?
- What would you do if you weren't so afraid of the idea of failing?

The place in my life where I observe creative intelligence unfolding with ease is in writing. I see so clearly that what flows on to the page usually comes through me before I even have a chance to consciously think it. We're continuously connected to creativity and our natural state is one of flow. When we don't hit the keyboard we get in the way of the magic. We don't transform the formless into form.

It may be we don't hit the keys in whatever form we feel called to create. Perhaps we're afraid of failing so we don't hit the piano keys. We may hit the keys at home but be terrified of performing in public and being visible.

Recently in a Living Fearlessly, Coaching Intensive with a client, the image which popped into my mind as we explored the nature of creative flow, was one of a switchboard operator.

The operator doesn't need to use physical strength or willpower to transfer calls. They only need to know which button to press, and to be present to press the buttons. Life can be as effortless as transferring calls when we do what's in front of us. All of the resources we'll ever need are available already. Most of us are so caught up in the past or the future we can't see 'the buttons' under our noses and as a result life feels very difficult.

As we understand more about how reality works, our awareness deepens and we begin to notice people, resources and opportunities. We didn't spot them before because we weren't present in the moment. Life is so much easier when we show up and respond to what shows up. There's a lot of confusion about how to attract good fortune. Like me, many people, have experimented with different practices and beliefs in an effort to bend reality to our will, in order to manifest what we want. The problem with this is it centres on us trying to control our circumstances which is impossible. Beyond our own interpretation of events, they are not within our control so it's a waste of precious energy.

Abundance is all around us so we don't need to chase it. We're always connected because we're made of creative intelligence. I read that we're made of stardust and so I became curious and wanted to learn more. Astronomer, Carl Sagan, said, 'We're made of star stuff.' He explained there are carbon, nitrogen and oxygen atoms in our bodies which were created in previous generations of stars over 4.5 billion years ago. It's amazing but true. We're all connected to the infinite potential of the universe no matter what our religion or philosophy.

When we relax enough to be in touch with our own intuition or inner guide, the hard work of trying to control everything so we can stop worrying, no longer makes sense. It's surplus to our needs. The misunderstanding which causes us to pile on self-created stress and pressure is one of attributing results solely to our own efforts. We'll explore this more deeply in the next chapter about puncturing the stress myth, but now let's look at how we can enjoy a more wonderful experience of life.

The 'Should-Do' Tape Stopped Playing

Due to the misunderstanding I had of how my mind worked I used to think it was up to me to try to turn off the dreaded voice of what's commonly known as the 'inner-critic.' No wonder it felt so hard. Having to monitor and edit our inner voice is a full-time job. It no longer makes sense to me to self-edit or try to manage my thoughts. I'm now able to impartially observe that they are mostly of no consequence to my life. If I choose to believe the thoughts which bring me down, the result is I instantly feel down. I've developed a taste for it. I identify a low mood for what it is; I've swallowed some polluted thoughts and temporarily lost sight of my wisdom as I wallow in them. We are not our thoughts and they only ever hold the meaning we make up about them. Even a glimmer of this understanding can transform our whole experience of life.

After my anxiety and 'morning dread' suddenly dissolved, I noticed the 'should-do' tape which had been running in my mind for as long as I can remember, suddenly stopped playing. I didn't consciously do anything to switch it off. I'd already seen how futile it is to try. Something incredible occurred without my intervention. It stopped and I only noticed it wasn't playing after several conversations with clients when we talked about their compulsion to work constantly. When not working, they think about what they should be doing and feel guilty. They rarely allow themselves a moment to enjoy life just as it is.

One client called it 'the monologue,' and said it played in his head continuously even when shopping. The only time he felt free of the nagging voice was when watching sport or 'losing himself' in interesting work. There's a familiar pattern in many of my coaching conversations. High achievers and high performers often believe if they aren't thinking about what they 'should' be doing, even when not doing it, they're lazy. It's as if they fear they won't be responsible enough to implement, unless their task list is permanently top of mind. It's exhausting when we operate this way because we don't allow ourselves any free mental bandwidth to recharge. We may not even be aware we have this 'script' running in our 'software.' After some time in this overthinking mode we begin to see it as normal.

Our electronic devices operate independently. We don't need to keep checking the plug is still connected to the mains. It's the same with us; we can function at optimum capacity without continuously checking our to-do list. When we see how counter-productive it is to incessantly be thinking about what we should be doing and instead begin to trust our self, it looks like insane behaviour. This is how my own guilty, 'should-do,' monologue ceased. I saw the madness and it fell away without effort.

We've been indoctrinated to believe hard work is virtuous ever since the industrial revolution. Factory owners wanted employees to work long, regular hours and so, 'Hard work gets you to heaven,' was preached in churches. The implication today is we still operate in accordance with the unhelpful belief there's a benefit to putting long hours in. People who get paid by the hour, week or month, are rewarded for their time. This isn't accurate or productive for self-employed people, entrepreneurs and business owners who create value through performance and results.

FREEDOM IS CLARITY OF MIND, NOT A RESULT

I've noticed many go-getters operate in the painful illusion of having to work all of the time to be successful. It means they never enjoy a minute of true mental freedom. The old saying, 'There's no rest for the wicked,' comes to mind. Many of my clients upon initially working with me, share that they not only worry about their productivity but also feel guilty when things do go well if they don't work really hard. It's as if the results don't count when it feels easy because they haven't suffered enough. Some of them ask, 'Is it okay to feel this good?'

THE MIND-BODY CONNECTION

When we believe we're lazy when not constantly working or thinking about work, not only do we burn through our mental bandwidth but we're also vulnerable to what's known as 'burn out.' From a young age I suffered from ailments, often labelled as stress related, such as anxiety, mouth ulcers, cold sores, dermatitis and immune system disorders. I thought I was prone to burn-out and needed to take extra good care of myself. These days it still seems sensible to take good care of myself but I no longer feel vulnerable to experiencing burn out, stress or exhaustion.

I appreciate the power of my own human resilience and as a result feel able to trust myself to know when to stop and take breaks. It's not a prescription, but rather an inner knowing of what's best in the moment. Only we can ever really know what's best for us. This is why recognising and trusting our own intuition and wisdom is the key to living fearlessly.

What's more likely to be going on when we feel exhausted is we've innocently misused our mind to the point where our body begins to feel the effects. Our mind needs to rest and if we indulge our busy mind over a long period of time it doesn't get a chance to refresh itself. I've seen this show up for me as both the physical symptoms of anxiety as well as fairly severe health issues. Many people suffer from chronic fatigue and other nervous related disorders which I believe can be greatly relieved by understanding the impact of a busy mind. The Three Principles understanding is sometimes referred to as the only solution needed to resolve all human problems. Although this may sound like hyperbole, I see more clearly everyday, how understanding our own minds takes us upstream to where every problem is initially created.

We can spend years of our life, feeling and believing our insecure thoughts and thinking we need to do something about them. Or we can give our self permission to be insecure when we're insecure and the insecure thoughts will pass. Feeling insecure at times, is a natural part of the human condition. It's like indigestion. When we get indigestion we panic and take medication. It usually won't be long before the medication agitates the problem because there are then more toxins in our system to digest.

We have digestive systems which are designed to flush out our body without any outside intervention and they do a really good job when we let them get on with it. If we keep adding unhealthy food into our digestive system, at some point the system will raise the alarm. The digestive system, like our mind, has a self-clearing function which rights itself when left to it's natural devices. We don't need to call the thought police.

TRUSTING OUR FEARLESS INTUITION

When we trust our fearless intuition, 'Superpower,' we naturally become the courageous leader of our life. We no longer feel alone. We're able to navigate with confidence, knowing we always have an inner satellite navigation system to guide us. The greater intelligence of the Universe has our back but when we don't trust we're connected to something much bigger and more powerful than our thoughts, we struggle, stress and strive.

We try to prove our self, and yearn to be the top dog in order to impress someone we care about so they will admire us. Notice how subtly this can show up in our thought patterns so we don't even know it's there. It's as if we're bound by invisible chains restricting all of our movements, not knowing we can be mentally free whatever our situation.

When we don't see something is present in our thoughts, it's a blindspot. This is why coaching; particularly Transformation Coaching is so impactful. We run around in our lives listening to our thoughts and thinking they are reality. We don't realise our minds work more like projectors than cameras and we see evidence of what we think everywhere. This is sometimes called 'confirmation bias,' which is defined as the tendency to interpret new evidence as confirmation of one's existing beliefs or theories. Even when we gain this new understanding of how we experience our separate realities from the inside-out, we still get caught out over and over.

As we wake up to the new awareness of how thought plays tricks on us it's easy to think we've understood it. But the human experience is one of believing our thoughts and repeatedly spinning in ego. We usually only see our blindspots when someone who has a deeper grounding of how it works, points them out. Until now we didn't know our blindspot was made of thought. We believed we had a 'real' problem. We thought it was the circumstances making us feel a certain way and forgot we experience our circumstances through our own filtered thinking.

No matter how bad our problems look in the form of the physical plane, our experience of them is 100% made of thought. Events occur. We filter them through our personal thinking and then we judge them. No matter how poor the hand we've been dealt, suffering is always optional.

WE ARE FREE NO MATTER WHAT OUR CIRCUMSTANCES

It's fascinating to think of extreme situations such as that of Viktor Frankl, Austrian neurologist, psychiatrist and author of 'Man's Search For Meaning.' Frankl was a Holocaust survivor and the book chronicles his experiences as an Auschwitz concentration camp inmate during World War II.

Frankl writes, 'Everything can be taken from a man but one thing: the last of the human freedoms — to choose one's attitude in any given set of circumstances, to choose one's own way.'

'When we are no longer able to change a situation, we are challenged to change ourselves.'

'Between stimulus and response there is a space. In that space is our power to choose our response. In our response lies our growth and our freedom.'

Frankl's wife, father, mother and brother died in the camps so the situation was dire by any standards but somehow he was able to see his own wellbeing and access his mental freedom.

We can't stop life unfolding but we can be present in the moment to make the most of what shows up. The truth is, nothing can permanently damage our psychology when we see we have innate mental health. Even people with serious mental health issues experience clarity some of the time. By pointing people towards their mental health they are more likely to see it, rather than believing they are permanently broken and need to be fixed.

The Frankl example puts everyday challenges into perspective. It's as if we think we can trick people into believing we're not human and we attempt to hide our vulnerability. It's a great relief to worry less about being judged. Whether we realise it or not, we all judge people through our judgemental personal thinking.

When we know we have access to mental freedom at all times we can be at peace with not knowing or having an answer for everything. Being at peace with not having to prove we're so smart, and have everything together is liberating. This is true freedom. We're free to be curious and open to hear something new instead of delving through our mental filing cabinet for old opinions to serve up to whoever will listen. This true freedom opens up a whole new way of life because we no longer need to be fearful of what people think.

THOUGHTS SUCH AS:

'What if the person I love doesn't love me?'

'What if the client doesn't hire me?'

'What if I receive negative feedback?'

'What if I mess up when I speak?'

'What if I don't create the level of success I crave?'

These type of fearful thoughts begin to lose their grip on us when we have the awareness to see that on the big rollercoaster of life they are simply a part of the ride. They don't define our self-worth as a human being.

WE CAN BE EFFORTLESSLY PRODUCTIVE

As the true nature of how humans tick continues to reveal itself to me, I see to what extent we get in our own way. We don't need to have all of the strategies and artificial boundaries we think we do to help us to be more productive. Fans of productivity systems, tend to love shortcuts or hacks. As I mentioned previously, I stumbled upon the best productivity shortcut I've seen in all of the years I've been studying productivity. It's very simple. It's about trusting our self to handle whatever shows up.

When we begin to really trust our self, we can drop all of the power moves, techniques and excessive preparation. There are so many ways we can save hundreds of hours every year once we trust our intuition. When we no longer entertain the idea we're going to create something perfect, for example, a presentation, we don't need to spend hours over-preparing. We can trust our inspiration, intuition or guidance will show up with us. We'll know what to do or say when we allow the space for something new to come through. We don't need to be up all night, agonising over how we're going to 'get it right.' There are many ways to get things right. Sleeping helps us to perform much better than overthinking and stressing does.

This saves potentially hundreds, if not thousands of hours throughout our career because we spend less time getting ready to get ready. This is a really practical side effect of the fearless principles. When we worry about how our presentation will be or how our client will respond to what we say, we try to predict the future. We can't. This is pure illusion.

All of the worrying and stressing is drastically reduced and gives us back hours of our life.

If we're not constantly preparing to be perfect, think of the hours available to create new, fresh ways to enjoy our life. When we're present to what's happening in the moment we have a clear mind and can experience the connection to something bigger than our self. This is where inspiration comes from and how new ideas pop into our mind 'out of the blue.' When our mind is quiet, it's as though we enjoy a stable Wi-Fi connection which is available to us on demand.

We've got access to the connection all of the time and it's there to give us beautiful insights and aha moments which are perfect for us. We can't hear them when we're busy preparing for something in the future, or fretting about the past. We don't know what's going to unfold and what's going to happen, but we try to manipulate the future as if we do. This has been a huge repeated insight for me. I no longer spend my time going in and out of my own internal monologue saying, 'I should get more done. I must prepare.'

By accepting our human nature, we're able to be effortlessly productive. This occurs through trusting ourselves and being present to what's showing up in our life, not what we fear might show up. I've saved hundreds of hours in journaling. This was one of the big practical shifts I shared with my coach when I was first introduced to this understanding. I stopped worrying so much about what's going on in my life, writing it out and thinking I need to work through it. No one told me to stop. It just stopped making sense to do it. I'm not saying there's anything wrong with journaling, but if at the end of each day we're no better off, it makes sense to ask, 'Is it productive or even helpful?'

I used to constantly try to beat the clock and wonder where my time went. Instead of attempting to analyse my spinning thoughts, I used my free time to write this book. These days if I journal, which is rare, it's usually to jot down a new idea rather than as time-consuming therapy. For me, also gone is the need to go through endless courses and how-to fix myself books. I'm much more able to see what I want now because my mind's clearer. I still have moments where I feel confused. It's called being human, but I'm aware I'll settle down soon. I know the uncomfortable feeling will pass quickly if I don't turn it into a big deal.

THE SECRET OF SUCCESS

I no longer think I need a quick fix-it magic bullet to tell me how to do something and to make everything all right. I'm not living in the illusion of someone else having all of the answers. I'm able to invest in training and coaching in a more pragmatic way. If I want to learn a new skill, then I'll do so, but the sense of desperation I so often see in others, has gone. When I feel inspired to do some personal development, I see it as embarking on a new adventure. We have our own in-built satellite navigation system. We know what's right for us better than anybody. This is such a big shift into living fearlessly. After thirty years of trying to fix myself, it's a beautiful gift. We discover the secret of success when we stop looking outside for all of the answers and settle down to find them right under our nose.

When we see we live in this simple misunderstanding of reality, we're able to effortlessly solve our own problems and be the fearless leader of our life. We either see there was never a problem, watch the problem dissolve, or enjoy the clarity to take the action we desire.

HERE'S A SUMMARY OF THE KEY POINTS IN THIS CHAPTER:

- Failure isn't fatal. It's a sign we've given something a

shot. The judgement is what we're scared of, so we protect ourselves by playing safe.

- Our internal 'should-do' monologue stops playing when we see how counter-productive it is to run this 'script.'
- Life can be as effortless as transferring calls when we do what's in front of us.
- When we trust our intuition, we naturally become the fearless leader of our life.
- We always have access to mental freedom no matter what our circumstances.
- We are effortlessly productive when we show up and respond to what shows up.

There's an 'insight' space below to journal any new thoughts that come through as you read:

_____

_____

_____

Next we'll explore the stress myth and how you don't need to be stressed even when you're busy.

7

PUNCTURING THE STRESS MYTH

Recently I was imagining what a very different world we'd live in if more people understood stress is internally produced through a misuse of our own mind. Stress isn't something which happens to us as a result of our circumstances. Feeling stressed comes from stressful thoughts, which instantly translates into a stressful experience.

This is controversial because it's revolutionary thinking about how our psychology works. It's a bit like hundreds of years ago, believing the world was flat and someone saying no matter how far we sailed we wouldn't fall off the edge. It's disruptive because in this case it's not how we've been taught to think about stress. As more people learn how their mind works, the more normal this understanding will seem. There's an epidemic of self-induced stress spreading through organisations; in schools, companies, government, business and anywhere there are people who believe stress is created through their circumstances.

WHAT'S ON OUR MIND DOESN'T IMPROVE OUR PERFORMANCE

Teachers who don't understand how their mind works, pass their own insecurity and experience of stress on to their students. The students; I've seen this first hand with my two daughters, are being prepared for life thinking they have to battle stress. They think feeling anxious, overwhelmed and stressed is a necessary requirement to perform well when there's a challenge i.e. an exam. It's not. It doesn't have to be. Our experience is one of whatever we feel in the moment and we don't need to hang on to feelings of stress.

Our performance in every endeavour is better when we have less on our mind. In fact, what's on our mind isn't of any consequence to the results we want to create. Children suffering acutely from the symptoms of anxiety and stress is due to parents and teachers not having an understanding of how our minds work. If we don't understand how our software works, it's impossible to teach how to operate it.

Consider a life without 'stress.' How amazing would it be? This is what's on offer when we begin to trust our intuition and be guided by our own wisdom. Living fearlessly doesn't ever require us to spin in our own fearful thoughts. We may find our self spinning but when we see how little it helps, we're less likely to indulge.

Stress is experienced when we believe our fearful thoughts. The symptoms caused by our frantic, busy mind do impact both our mental clarity and physical functions. A few years ago my dear brother who always had such a zest for life, died suddenly of a heart attack at the age of forty-eight. One day we were chatting on the phone and the next he was gone. He'd been complaining of feeling stressed ever since the recession when his company crashed. Almost overnight he went from having multi-million pound revenues, to struggling to pay his creditors. He increasingly felt his circumstances were beyond his control. His stressful experience came from trying to fight reality to regain control.

His financial situation was precarious for a number of years and his health deteriorated. I'm grateful he visited us a couple of days before he died. I remember being shocked by how laboured his breathing was. He was so out of breath he could barely make it up the high street. In the years leading up to his death, he attributed stress to his financial situation and attempted to manage his moods and anxious feelings by distracting himself. His distractions included smoking and gambling. While these types of activities often feel pleasurable at the time, as we all know, they're extremely addictive.

WE CAN NEVER GET ENOUGH OF OUR ADDICTION

The nature of addiction is one of never being able to get enough. When we can never get enough it's a vicious circle because we indulge our habit. We enjoy the temporary high and then come crashing back down to our version of reality. This is true, whatever our addiction. The cycle then begins all over again as we crave more. There's no lasting satisfaction when we're addicted to an activity or a substance. There's no solution to a feeling so trying to numb the pain never provides permanent relief.

'Whenever we feel stressed out, that's a signal that our brain is pumping out stress hormones. If sustained over months and years, those hormones can ruin our health and make us a nervous wreck.'

— DANIEL GOLEMAN

For years I drank alcohol as a way to try to escape my anxious feelings. I think many people drink alcohol in an attempt to relax. Many of the older members of my family drank quite heavily and I grew up thinking it was normal. What I hadn't realised was how dependent we can become on alcohol as a prop in social situations. If we feel nervous or awkward at social events it's tempting to drink more than usual. I knew something wasn't right in my believing I needed to drink alcohol to feel better, but all around me people seeming to be drinking.

When I first arrived in Jerusalem, I was amazed by how few people drank alcohol regularly. I worked in several pubs and restaurants and often the girls would order diet coke or a dessert and the guys would order a beer and a snack. Many didn't drink alcohol at all and it wasn't because it's against the Jewish religion. They didn't seem to need to drink to be more gregarious. It wasn't a cultural norm. I became fascinated with the sociable Israeli culture and what I now recognise as the innate self-confidence we all possess beneath our insecurity. At age eighteen this seemed very different to me than my experience of British binge drinking and a social calendar in the bank, revolving around pubs and opportunities to drink. In Jerusalem I would go out with my friends and we'd party a lot but I noticed a different energy around their relationship with drinking.

Every culture seems to have its addictions and in Israel many people tend to smoke and gamble. Interestingly, these days I've noticed they also drink more than back then, probably due to being widely exposed to western drinking culture. Ironically now I no longer drink, when I go on holiday there seem to be drinking opportunities everywhere. For years I wished I could give up my white wine habit and became very strict about only drinking at weekends because one glass seemed to lead to another. One of the side-effects of drinking I most disliked was the inevitable hangover. When we fall into cycles of anxious thinking, stress or low moods, they usually feel much worse with a hangover. A hangover only intensified my 'morning dread' and so repeatedly I'd swear to give up drinking. I would abstain for a few weeks and then be back on the white wine at the next social event.

After numerous attempts to give up it was a series of events which finally led to the ditching of my white wine habit. Around this time my father was very sick with a rare and seemingly undiagnosable auto-immune system disease. The doctors didn't know what caused it and didn't know what to do for him. He was frequently in a lot of pain. He was advised to stop drinking, which for a sociable person like my father who lived for his daily get-together at the pub, was a bitter blow. He was plied with steroids and suffered from the severe effects on his body.

I visited him in hospital and helped to bring him home but he wasn't in a good way. Even in the high temperatures of Spain he shivered as I hugged him in the hospital and could find no respite. It was heart-breaking and there seemed little we could do. I had to get back to my young family in England. One week before Christmas my brother called to tell me our father had been rushed back into hospital after keeling over. The Spanish doctor said he had 'poison on the brain.' We had no idea what it meant or what was going on and both felt very helpless. All of the London airports were snowed in with no flights leaving for Alicante and I was unable to drive north to fly with my brother due to the snowy conditions en route. I received another call shortly before midnight and heard my Dad's voice. He was about to go into the operating theatre and was lucid enough to say, 'I love you Rackie,' which was his nickname for me. I could barely reply and curled up in a ball on my bed sobbing quietly for most of the night. My brother said the surgeon predicted there was only a small chance of him making it because of his history of heavy drinking. They didn't think his body was strong enough to survive the operation. I can't remember exactly when I heard the news but I already knew in my heart he was gone. Sometime during the early hours of the next morning I received confirmation he'd not made it.

I hadn't planned on writing about this tragic event but it seems relevant in sharing the impact addiction can have on our life. We may not think our habit is addictive because we see it as 'social.' I know many people who believe their stress is alleviated by drinking alcohol and so they become increasingly dependent and often 'need a drink.' When we drink to try to heal the wounds, escape stress or fill our self up, it's a painful void which can never be filled through addiction.

I stopped drinking a few months before my father died. I was increasingly dissatisfied with my drinking experience and one night in August we'd been out for 'a drink.' I'd had two or three glasses of wine at the pub and before I'd even finished the final one I felt anxious and unhappy. It no longer made sense to me to drink to relieve 'stress' when the drinking itself seemed to be causing the stress.

Now I understand how our minds work, I can see my thoughts about drinking were ruining my enjoyment. I didn't sleep much in the night and had a sense of knowing my drinking days were coming to an end. I declared a year of no drinking because it seemed less of a big leap than saying, 'I'm giving up forever.' It seemed lighter and more achievable to commit to one year and see how it went. I read, 'No More Hangovers,' by Allen Carr which is a terrific little book and after the second reading I felt less and less inclined to want to drink. I had begun by drinking less frequently and one Friday, which was traditionally the day I enjoyed a few drinks, I went to the local shop and came back with 'The Bruce Lee Story' instead. I hadn't bought a bottle of wine. It felt like a big deal and did require some willpower but I was pleased.

When I heard my Dad might have survived the operation if he'd not been a drinker, something clicked within me. I felt a new resolution to not go back to my old ways. By my late thirties I wouldn't have been classed as a heavy drinker and even when I was younger I didn't drink on a daily basis. But I had a suspicion that my experience would be better without this addictive habit.

The year turned into two and as I write, it's now seven years since my last glass of wine. I'm often asked why I don't drink and I have a range of answers depending on my mood. Health is an important one. As I mentioned earlier, I had suffered with a variety of stress-related conditions and after seeing what happened to my father's health I had no wish to continue down the same road. It's common to believe alcohol is a stress reliever but it's a depressant. The feeling of not being able to have enough was something I felt keenly in drinking alcohol. I enjoyed a temporary buzz and then it felt like it was all downhill from there.

SOMETHING SHIFTED WITHIN ME

What I can see with the perspective of time and through this new understanding is something shifted deep within me. I thought reading the book made the difference, but I've recommended the same book to many people and don't think any of them have completely given up drinking. It's not the book; it's what we see for ourselves as we read. Of course, reading about the details of how alcohol can impact our health, may inspire us to drink less. For me it was a culmination of events, experiences and insights which meant when I finally gave up drinking I didn't require any willpower. Now it seems unlikely I'll drink again, at least to the point where I can't think clearly. This doesn't require much for most of us. I don't want to go through my life feeling numb, so drinking doesn't seem at all helpful in my desire to live a more conscious life. Stopping drinking was a big turning point for me which helped me to begin facing the reality of my anxious thinking rather than masking it with alcohol.

Currently I'm aware of the habit of frequently checking my phone. This might not seem like a serious addiction and I know I'm not alone. Most people in the modern world seem to be glued to their phones and social media. My experience of this addiction is mostly pleasurable because of the instant gratification, but it's common to suffer when we don't receive the message we want. When we don't understand our experience is created from the inside-out, it's clear why billions of people feel anxious, stressed and even depressed when others don't interact with them in the way they believe they should. No matter how many times we check, we'll never find our self-worth in our phone.

This experience of living through our virtual reality is a great reminder of how we always live in our own thought created world. In the online scenario, not only do we filter people and events through our personal thinking, we also attempt to construct reality through snippets of fast-moving information coming at us in multiple formats. No wonder so many people feel stressed and overwhelmed. Our mind speeds up like a fan on an overheated computer and is unable to process effectively, so we begin to shut down. If we feel depressed when looking at social media feeds, this could be why.

A BUSY MIND THRIVES ON DISTRACTION

When we think our wellbeing comes from 'out there,' it makes sense to believe what's online is real. What we see is only our interpretation of the words or images. Our moods can be subject to what we see on our social media feed. If we're in a network of people who value being 'positive,' it can look as though everyone has a perfect life. If things are going well for us, we feel happy for them but what about when they're not? If our mood is high, life feels good but when our mood is low, we see everything through our low mood filter. Nearly everyone in business on my social media feeds seems to be having big wins and looking ever more attractive, with images posted through a photographic filter. In pops one image and out pops an enhanced one. This is similar to how we filter our experience. How we react depends entirely on our state of mind in the moment, which is always helpful to know. A busy mind thrives on distraction and we can be lost in a thought storm for hours or days. It can feel particularly depressing when we don't understand what's happening.

In my brother's situation I wish I'd then had this understanding of how stress is manufactured from within. Perhaps I could have helped him to see how his experience was being created. By pointing to the truth of how believing his dark thoughts exacerbated his situation, he could have slowed down mentally. He would then have been able to access clarity of mind which is where solutions to business and money problems are found. It's too late now and I'll never know. When we seek relief through addictive activities there's often a steep price to be paid.

EACH DAY THE CLOCK RESETS TO ZERO FOR STRIVING HIGH ACHIEVERS

I was deep in conversation with a client about the nature of high performance and how we get in our own way. We talked about his tendency to practice self-flagellation with stressful thinking and how it never helps even though he believed it motivated him. I could see clearly how no matter what he achieved, and he'd achieved some pretty amazing milestones in business, he could never meet his own standards.

I've noticed this pattern as regular practice for striving high achievers. Each day the clock resets to zero and we don't feel worthy or quite good enough. And so the race begins all over again. It's like Groundhog Day; a bit of a nightmare until we wake up. The great news is we all have the innate ability to wake up. When we live our lives with this erroneous thought pattern, we steal our own peace of mind. I felt sad because I could see he was missing out on the joy of the experience of being the wonderful person he is. Others saw his genius shine through but he continually doubted himself.

My experience was similar. I had never been able to measure up to my own standards no matter how much praise I received. In a flash I saw how stark the contrast was to the way I operate now. I hadn't appreciated the transformation in the processing of my achievements until then. Sometimes through seeing how others perceive life we're able to see what's shifted profoundly for us. When change happens effortlessly as it does through personal insight, it doesn't always arrive to the sound of marching bands and tambourines. We may miss it initially.

During our conversation he didn't yet see clearly how thinking he was not productive enough wasn't true, but was self-judgement. Even when we've experienced big insights in other areas of our life we still often think problems are real and not our perception. I gave him several nudges in the direction of truth so he could begin to glimpse more. Then I let go and trusted his mind would settle and at some point he would experience new thought. He did. Insights don't arrive on demand and sometimes the more we struggle to 'get it,' the less likely our mind seems to reveal something fresh. This is because we're churning old thought in our minds, trying to intellectually figure it out. What seems to be much more conducive to insight is being in a quiet reflective state with little on our mind.

This may be why some people don't think they've experienced an insight yet. We could be experiencing fresh thoughts but not have the level of awareness to notice. The more we think about what we don't have, the more likely we are to create a stressful experience. When we relax and trust we have the capacity for new thought, insight pops into our mind in its own time. Although we can't order insights on demand, when they come they often rock our world. The tremors may feel small or large and be instant or more of an aftershock but they shift our consciousness so we see reality more clearly.

Shortly after this conversation he experienced some big insights and shared how he saw his new worldview through a wonderful analogy about railway carriages. In the first carriage were his thoughts about problems, issues and challenges, in the corridor linking to the next carriage were feelings of anxiousness, stress, self-doubt and fear. He saw that staying in the corridor was an unpleasant, painful experience. There was nothing to hold on to, the ground was unstable and feelings seemed to spin out of control.

In the next carriage lay limitless solutions, peace of mind, answers, options, activity and production. He realised before his insight, he'd spent a lot of time in the corridor, oblivious to the truth that there wasn't any value in being there. Now he sees there's no need to stay in the gap where fear and stress live and instead proceeds directly to the carriage of infinite creative potential.

It's important to be clear, this is someone's personal insight and how they see it. Our view of how our experience works may look completely different. When underpinned by the principles I'm pointing to, we can be confident we're moving in the direction of finding solid ground. My client could now see how he didn't need to spend any time in the 'stress' corridor and could proceed directly to the second carriage. I laughed because it reminded me of a 'When Harry Met Sally,' moment; in this case with a 'I'll have what he's having,' because his insights continued to pop effortlessly.

In this example the first carriage is a great analogy for the level of consciousness we have around our current situation. The corridor represents the impact of feeling one's thinking or being lost in fearful thought. The second carriage reveals a beautiful spaciousness of Infinite Creative Potential or Universal Mind. We can experience the principles in action without needing to intellectually learn them.

Suffering around goal-setting is common with high achievers because when we're very goal driven we tend to focus on the goals we don't hit, not the ones we do. Traditional coaching encourages goal-setting as a way to help the client be accountable to move forward with their vision. The reason I no longer work in this way is because when we see we already have everything we need within us, it makes no sense to measure progress by where we need to get to. Meeting goals can only ever occur in the future so isn't particularly helpful in living fearlessly in the present. In an upcoming chapter we'll talk about playing the game of business and how goals can be a fun way to enjoy the game when we play on solid ground.

To puncture the stress myth I want to point to the link between stress and measuring our success by goals. If we put a lot of value on meeting our goals, by default we focus on our poor performance when we don't meet them. I've noticed many high performers are so focussed on their missed goals they completely forget about those they hit.

HERE ARE SOME GOAL-SETTING COACHING QUESTIONS:

- Do you always find a reason to move the goal-post?
- Are there goals you've hit which seemed critical but upon hitting them you felt empty?
- When you reach a goal do you celebrate or are you straight back into the next goal?
- Where do you think your ability to hit goals comes from?

It's funny because so many people barely acknowledge their success when they hit a goal. They wear their 'didn't hit the goal goggles' so when they hit one it barely registers on their goal hitting scale. We may find our self thinking, 'Well I only hit this goal because ...' There's often a way we minimise our achievement and so we never reach our destination. Conversely if we celebrate and make a fuss of hitting our goals, perhaps because we've heard it's important to celebrate our success, it can leave us feeling hollow. Thoughts like, 'It was a fluke, I'm not sure I'll ever be able to repeat it,' are common. Most extremely successful and gifted people don't understand where their genius comes from and so they doubt their ability to repeat or sustain it.

I experience goals in a completely different way now. It's not a case of not giving credit where it's due but more an understanding of how it's not all on us anyway. When we believe we're on our own and 'stress' and 'pressure' rest on our shoulders, high performance can feel like a heavy weight to bear. Once we spot how ego wants our success to be all about our own efforts, we're free to enjoy an effortless experience of missing and hitting goals. We're safe in the knowledge that invisible forces are at play assisting us. What we point our goal-goggles at is beyond our control anyway. We only need to show up and respond to what shows up to fully play our part.

It's not that I don't acknowledge my efforts but more about me seeing how much easier life is when I'm not spinning in the stress corridor. I no longer spend much time trying to figure out how to hit goals and control the Universe. Trust plays a big part in surrendering to the great unfolding of life. As we travel on the 'Living Fearlessly' journey, we see beautiful new sights as we pass through unchartered terrain. When we give ourselves all of the credit for our achievements, we naturally deduct points when we don't get the result we want. This often leads to beating ourselves up. We're now working upstream from tactics and strategies and when we see the truth of who we are, we don't need to pat ourselves on the back to remind ourselves we're worthy.

We don't do our best work when we believe our efforts are never enough. By harshly critiquing our performance even when we do brilliant work, we puncture the air from our own tyres. When we see this for ourselves a whole world of fearless flow opens up to us to replace our exhausting life of stressful striving.

———

HERE'S A SUMMARY OF THE KEY POINTS IN THIS CHAPTER:

- Stress doesn't come from our circumstances. We manufacture it from the inside-out.
- Our performance is always better when we're not pre-occupied with what's on our minds.
- The nature of addiction is one of never being able to get enough.
- Self-confidence is innate in all human beings and exists beneath the surface of our insecurities.
- A busy mind thrives on distraction until we stop feeding it.
- Striving high achievers are rarely satisfied with their performance. They begin each day at zero when they don't understand how their mind works.
- We're free to enjoy an effortless experience of missing and hitting goals.

There's an 'insight' space below to journal any new thoughts that come through as you read:

_____

_____

_____

Next we'll explore creating from infinite potential.

PART III

LIVING FEARLESSLY

8

CREATING FROM INFINITE POTENTIAL

'I'm gonna put 100 songs in your pocket. No, 500, I'm gonna put between 500 and 1000 songs in your pocket.'

I found the story of Steve Jobs so inspiring, and loved when he made this pledge to his daughter, Lisa. She carried a Walkman and he predicted a whole new music delivery system in the form of the iPod. I don't know if the idea was already percolating in his mind or if it was sparked by seeing his daughter with the Walkman.

Whatever the case, new ideas pop into our minds exactly in this way. One minute there's nothing; and the next, a brand new possibility we couldn't envision before. This is how invention and innovation reveal themselves. We don't need to be like Steve Jobs to have a good idea, but creators like him seem to be naturally attuned to the unknown. It's as if they have an open, clear channel, whilst many of us operate with a blocked channel populated with self-doubt. If Steve Jobs had taken his personal psychology seriously, I wouldn't be writing this book on my computer. He didn't seem to have been a particularly well balanced individual but it didn't prevent him from being inspired. Our state of mind in any particular moment doesn't need to stop us from being inspired either.

We Have The Innate Capacity To Receive Creative Ideas

Once we know how the system works we seem to be more available to receive fresh, new ideas. Some may already be coming our way but we may miss them when they knock on our mental door. Receiving incredible ideas in the form of 'insights' isn't something only available to an elite few. As we see more about 'Living Fearlessly' we naturally open up to new possibilities. All of us have the innate capacity to receive creative ideas in the form of insights or inspiration.

Sometimes insights come clothed as no-brainer next steps, and we barely notice them. We operate this way seamlessly throughout most of our lives. A thought occurs to us and we either act on it or not. Either way another thought soon appears because there's no scarcity in the thought department. It's a little bit like waiting for a bus. It may seem an age until one arrives but it's often only a few minutes. As the bus pulls into the stop, another often follows closely behind. The second bus travels the same route so if there are more empty seats we might hop on. We have the free will to act on whichever thoughts we want, in the same way we choose which bus to board. It may not always feel this way because thoughts can be so compelling, but it's true.

Other times, insights create huge ripples and have a lasting impact on our lives. The impact differs but the insight delivery system is predictable. In earlier chapters I frequently pointed towards Universal Mind which I see as a giant pool of infinite creative potential. Many people are aware of this creative energy. I'd like to offer a new way of seeing this force at work in our life. This Universal energy flows through us all and is how we're all connected. In spirituality this is sometimes known as 'the oneness.' I suggest it's less important to label the energy, but reassuring to know there's a creative flow running through each of us. This force sparks our human engine and lights us up.

When streams of inspiration flow freely into our mind from the giant pool, we become the Principles of Mind, Consciousness and Thought, in action. The Principles, when working together, work as one. In the example of receiving a new idea, mind serves a new thought up, as if to say, 'Hi Rachel. What do you think about this one? Is this of interest to you?' If my consciousness or awareness is low when the idea floats in, I'm liable to dismiss it as not useful to my business or life. I may miss it completely if I don't have the mental clarity for it to register on my radar.

One of my favourite books about creativity is, 'Big Magic,' by Elizabeth Gilbert, the author of 'Eat, Pray, Love.' She shares a fascinating account of how she believes ideas circulate and land in different people's minds at the same time. Sometimes we're ready for them and we take action. Other times the ideas move on when they're not implemented. She tells the story of how after commencing work on a novel, she lost momentum and the project lay unfinished. Soon after, she met a friend who shared her new book idea with her. It was almost identical. It seems as though nobody's ideas are their own unless they act on them and turn them from the formless into form. Even then we often see similar inventions and innovations appearing simultaneously. Sometimes one is inspired by another but many times ideas seem to simply land, and look for a receptive home. The creator transforms their ideas into reality by acting on their inspiration instead of indulging self-doubt. The person who struggles is stuck in the murky ripples of the pool rather than waiting for the surface to settle, and for clear, sparkling water to emerge.

How New Ideas Are Hatched

Recently I spotted an infographic shared by Barclays Bank which showed statistics of where entrepreneurs in the UK hatch their new business ideas. 19% get them on the train, 32% in bed, 19% out in nature, 19% drinking coffee and 14% in the shower. For some reason these add up to 103% which is odd, but we get the picture. The reason I'm sharing these statistics is to point to the source of fresh, new ideas. They can land at any time and it's beyond our control.

Many of us have heard of the concept of good ideas arriving when we're in the shower. It's not much of a stretch of the imagination to believe good ideas come when we're in the shower and so we had better take lots of showers. The problem with this misunderstanding of how life works is the shower was never the source of new ideas. When our mind settles, we're more likely to receive new thought, insights and ideas. We could be dancing, watching T.V, eating, at the cinema, walking the dog, showering, drifting off to sleep or any other number of activities, when our next big idea strikes. The point being it's not the place or activity which facilitates the arrival of the idea, but the receptivity of our mind.

We could be doing any of the aforementioned activities, be fully absorbed and enjoy wonderful mental clarity or have a very busy mind and not be present in the moment. Like a spinning fan it's considerably more difficult for something to get through the fast moving cracks than when the fan is static. But even then, ideas are able to filter through occasionally.

I'm often surprised when I reach my destination in the car and don't remember any of the details of the journey. Sometimes I can barely recall which route I took because I was so lost in thought. We often drive through life on auto-pilot because we're so distracted. When our minds are quietly reflective we're more open to inspiration striking than when we're trying to figure stuff out in a thought storm. When we hear entrepreneurs, creatives and business people recount their success stories we often hear them share their original plan. If we listen closely we hear how the journey really unfolded. It's very rare for the unfolding to match the original plan. This doesn't seem to stop us from thinking we're in the driver's seat and it's down to us to clear the roads.

It's often the same with their big idea; they talk of how it appeared one day 'out of the blue.' They may be living in the illusion that they figured it out but what probably happened was a solution or idea occurred to them. Millions of people experience exactly the same phenomenon but because they don't recognise how their mind works they ignore it. It seems to me we often take our insecure, fearful thinking much more seriously than our inspirational, intuitive guidance. This is why life so often feels like something we need to actively do. When we're attuned to our intuitive guidance it's enough to be present and follow our creative nudges to see where they lead. There's no guarantee the next one will be the 'big idea.' But we are likely to tilt the odds in our favour when we follow our nudges from the Universal giant pool. Wallowing in insecure thinking about why other people get all of the big breaks is unlikely to lead to inspired creation.

WE ALL POSSESS MAGIC SUPERPOWERS

We all possess 'Magic Superpowers.' They're built-in to our system and we don't find these superpowers outside of ourselves. Life unfolds from the inside-out and we get access to advanced mental software and a cutting-edge human operating system to make the most of our journey.

We have many innate superpowers but there are four which I particularly love to share because they're so key to high performance and living fearlessly. When we become aware of our superpowers we begin to spot them already in action. What I point towards is already at work in our life. It can be like receiving the latest gadget and not having any idea how to make use of all of the incredible features. Many people go through their lives only using the minimum capacity of their human potential. They're unaware there are advanced features available to them if only they knew which buttons to push.

THE SUPERPOWERS

INSIGHT - Is the innate capacity for new thought and understanding which all humans have built-in to their factory settings. When we're stuck, there's always a misunderstanding of how life works. Once we have insight into how insight works, it's simpler to spot when it comes our way.

INTUITION - Feels certain, clear and simple. As we develop our taste for intuition we begin to trust our gut instinct. There's a gentle knowing which guides us through life when we let it.

CREATIVE INTELLIGENCE - Is the energy behind life which runs through us from Universal mind. Creative Intelligence powers the whole system and is an abundant, unlimited force always available to us. This unlimited energy often shows up in our experience as insight, inspiration, creativity, flow or intuition.

RESILIENCE - Is like a reliable safety net. When we begin to notice how resilient we all are, it's natural for our trust of ourselves and others to deepen. We can't control what happens, but knowing we have an incredible inner-strength which rises up in times of crisis and emergency can be wonderfully comforting.

We all have access to this Transformation Toolkit in our factory settings. This is very encouraging and helps us to relax into living fearlessly without feeling the fear.

UNIVERSAL GENIUS

Leonardo da Vinci is a famous historical example of creative intelligence flowing through a clear channel to create amazing works in the world. Such was Leonardo's gift for creation he's known as a 'Renaissance Man' or 'Universal Genius.' Not only did he paint one of the most famous portraits of all time; 'The Mona Lisa,' he had many passions driven by his curiosity for how things worked.

Similar to Sir Isaac Newton, he was a polymath whose areas of interest included sculpting, invention, painting, science, music, mathematics, architecture, literature, engineering, geology, anatomy, astronomy, writing and botany. He's been called the father of Palaeontology and is considered one of the greatest painters of all time.

It seems as though Leonardo had access to the great quantum computer of creative intelligence and was able to tap into a vision of possibility which was hundreds of years ahead of others. His technological ingenuity was such that he conceptualised flying machines and concentrated solar power amongst other inventions seemingly not of their time.

What might be possible when we begin to grasp the potential of our personal connection to this flow of creative energy? The only obstacle to receiving innovative ideas is when we block this universal power by getting lost in our troubled, insecure thinking. This means we can enjoy flow and creativity even when we've labelled our self as someone who isn't creative. We are all creative beings and our superpowers make life easier when we understand we already have everything we need to live a happy life.

Recently I posted a question to my readers as part of my research for this book. The feedback was fascinating so I'll share the common fears, as well as my conclusion.

The question I asked was, "What would you say is the No.1

mindset 'block' or fear which you feel stops you from either doing what you want in life or business, or from reaching your highest potential?"

UNIVERSAL FEARS

- Fear of failure
- Fear of being vulnerable
- Fear that I have to do everything alone
- Fear of being visible
- Fear of wasted effort and no results
- Fear of not being enough
- Fear of physical pain
- Fear of judgement
- Fear of success
- Fear of looking stupid
- Fear of being reprimanded
- Fear of going to hell
- Fear of being embarrassed
- Fear of burning out
- Fear of not being able to cope

I gave people an option to send me a personal message so they didn't need to post their biggest fear in public in case they felt uncomfortable. Several shared their fears with me privately. It was interesting to note only two courageous men posted to share their fear. Most of the public posts were made by women. Twice the number of women as men, suffer from anxiety related fears and phobias according to a statistic I read.

I don't know how accurate this is but it could be why fewer

men posted. However I think it's more likely that many men see their fears as a weakness and think they should 'man up,' and get on with living. And there's something to be said for just getting on with it. Women, and I'm aware I'm generalising here, seem to be more open to sharing their fears. Perhaps this is because we're socially conditioned and applauded for being soft and feminine.

While all of these fears look individual, I noticed they're all rooted in the same insecurity. We all sometimes fear we're not good enough. This seems to be a universal 'human' fear. It's not a 'insert your name' fear. We all want to be understood, loved and accepted unconditionally. We all want to feel special. This complicates our experience of life because we can get lost in ego as we yearn to be recognised as unique.

All of us are special and at the same time we're all ordinary. I've loved waking up to the psycho-spiritual principles of how our experience really works because it's allowed me to embrace my ordinary humanity. Once we accept our ordinary human nature, we're free to rest in our big fearless self. There's nothing to do to be fearless; it's our natural state. It only changes when we believe our fearful thoughts.

All humans are special because we're all connected to the infinite creative potential of the universe and so I now see it as ordinary to be special. When we believe our fears, we think they are real. We can't choose which thoughts pop into our mind. We may be relieved to discover this because it's one less thing to attempt to control. When we forget that we each live in our own thought created reality, we lose sight of our power and the truth of who we are.

The truth is we 'think' we suffer from whatever fear we've labelled our self with. We are not our thoughts. We are not our fears. We are creative potential.

PROBLEM SOLVING FROM THE INFINITE POTENTIAL

When we tire of thinking what to do, we can choose to stop. When we start to have less respect for the intellect, our mind has a chance to refresh itself. It's designed to present us with solutions. Some of us have a tendency to micromanage our mind and try and jump in there to push things along. We think we need to figure everything out. This is a bit like manually pushing an expensive Ferrari uphill. Our mind is perfectly designed to present us with the solutions we need when we quieten down enough to allow it to function.

I think of our minds as being like a universal filing cabinet. We've got information and data collected over the years and it's been filed away in our cabinet. We may have invested a lot of money and time into collecting more knowledge to file in our cabinet. Perhaps we pride our self on our great intellectual understanding. Many of the high achievers I've worked with in recent years are this way. When a problem arises they begin to frantically rummage through the filing cabinet. If the problem is of a linear nature such as an analytical type dilemma, they may find the answer.

If the problem is of a nature they haven't encountered before, they usually struggle to find a solution in the outdated files. When I point them in the direction of the giant pool of infinite creative potential, they gain access to new files and data which they've never accessed before. It's like the difference between being restricted to working on your computer with no internet connection or being able to go online for new ideas. We all have access to the quantum filing cabinet and our wifi connection is always on, even when it feels as though we're offline.

When we keep trying to access old files to find new solutions it often ends in frustration. When we experience something that seems like a problem, we can move it to the back burner. We can walk away and do something else. By changing focus, we give our self mental space. Churning through stale information can lead to feeling impatient when we can't figure out an instant solution. Our flow of thoughts speeds up. Even though we've been taught to problem solve in this way, it's not the key to being effortlessly productive.

Fast thinking is not the fastest route to clarity and new solutions. By figuratively shoving a dilemma on the back burner, we usually see something new. It may be there for a week, a month or a year. We don't know. This is so helpful in stepping away and allowing our mind to do what it's designed for. It can come up with wonderful, new insights to serve up to us which we can't see when we're stuck in the busy mind of 'I must figure it all out now. I'm supposed to know the answers and I need to take urgent action.'

> 'Sometimes the questions are complicated and the answers are simple.'
>
> — Dr. Seuss

No matter how stuck we feel or how bad our situation looks at any given moment, we always have the potential for infinite creativity. This shows up as a fresh thought or realisation ... whatever we want to call it. It's always available to us in the same way a tap is connected to the water mains even when turned off. We can turn it on and off manually whenever we want but it's always ready to flow if we let it.

We have a real talent for getting in the way of our natural flow by overthinking how things should be. It's not that the flow isn't always there — it's simply that we mess with it. We try to control the flow like we might if we were messing with the water pipes. When the water mains has been turned off and back on, the tap often shudders and shakes before a steady flow resumes. And there ends the metaphor. We are not taps. We don't need to mess with our mains (minds) as they do a beautiful job of fixing themselves. We don't even need a plumber because we have our own built-in switch to innate mental health on a default setting.

How wonderful is this to know? We think we need to get in there when we feel blocked so we can make the flow happen. Or we jump in to try to lessen the flow when life feels, 'too full on,' 'out of control,' or 'over the top.' When we attempt to manage our experience because we think our little mind knows best, we're liable to do some damage trying to fix something that either:

a) Doesn't need fixing

b) Limits our creative potential by slowing down the flow of what wants to come through.

Two Possible Paths

I like to think of our experience of life as two possible paths we can travel. High achievers and those who label themselves as Type A people are especially proactive in micromanaging their experience. We feel out of control when we don't. I'm still a work in progress on this. In our innocence of wanting to be on the 'make it happen path,' we miss out on much of the effortless flow of life available when we allow our self to travel the 'flowing path.'

The wonderful news is, we are infinitely creative. We don't even need to think of ourselves as creative to be a creator. We don't need permission to create. We are a creation and we create every minute of the day. We may not like the experience of what we're creating which is when we're most likely to jump in and try to fix it. I'm not talking about law of attraction here. We don't control what happens although we may think we are manipulating events. When this is the case we're likely to blame ourselves when things don't go as planned.

We're only ever experiencing our perception of what's happening. This is why knowing we're sitting in infinite creative potential can instantly give wonderful relief. Our experience can change at any moment. There's nothing to do but to see it. This means we can stop beating ourselves up. It's frustrating but so many of us do it. We're so tough on ourselves. We think we're supposed to know the answers to everything. This isn't how it works. We can step away. When we change the channel we see something new. It may not be the full solution in one massive download. As our mind settles we're able to get more of a sense of possibility all around us.

These days I have such respect for a quiet mind. I didn't

understand how it worked before. I knew I didn't feel happy when I was thinking a lot but I didn't know mental freedom is available to us all of the time. When our mind is quiet, we're more able to see what's right in front of us. Developing respect for a quiet mind means we're more likely to cultivate one. When we see there's no benefit to manic paced thinking, we naturally do less of it. It feels exhausting once we wake up to the difference between mental clarity and a busy mind.

———

HERE'S A SUMMARY OF THE KEY POINTS IN THIS CHAPTER:

- We don't need to be like Steve Jobs to have a good idea. Unlimited, fresh, creative ideas are available to us all.
- It's not the place or activity which facilitates the arrival of a new idea, but the receptivity of our mind.
- We all possess innate superpowers and when we're aware of them it's like unlocking the advanced features of our software.
- Universal fears are all rooted in the same insecure thinking.
- We don't usually find new ideas in old files.
- We are not taps. We don't need to mess with our mains.
- Developing a respect for a quiet mind, cultivates one.

There's an 'insight' space below to journal any new thoughts that come through as you read:

_____

Next I'll share what I've seen about living full out and fearlessly.

9

FULL OUT AND FEARLESS

There's a wonderful freedom available to us all in our life, work or business, when we see our past doesn't define our present or future experience. It's not uncommon to feel weighed down by what we see as our failures. It's as if we think we need to carry our past, which is a heavy load, on our shoulders. It's no wonder our experience of life can feel tortuous and difficult. What we need most, to be effective in every area of our lives, is presence in the moment.

When our heads are stuck in the past, we're not present, which means we're unlikely to perform well. Once we begin to appreciate we have innate superpowers and advanced software at our disposal, we can build on this new solid ground to create what we want.

What comes to mind as I write this, is forgiving ourselves for whatever we've done or not done in the past. We can always begin again with a clean slate. Living Fearlessly isn't about following other people's prescriptions. I'm no longer an advocate of complex techniques for us to work on forgiveness. Forgiving can be simple. Transformation occurs through personal insight even when it looks as if it's a result of ritual. Forgiving works the same way as every other feeling.

THE PROBLEM WITH BEING A SEEKER

A wonderful feeling of peace can always be found within us. This is great news because there's nothing to do to be forgiven other than to let our mind settle and be present in this moment. There may be times in our lives where we swirl about in unforgiving thoughts. They arise from our insecurity in the moment, in the way other fearful thoughts appear. They soon pass when we don't insist on hanging on to them tightly as if they have real meaning. I did a lot of forgiveness work on my spiritual journey and whilst it can be soothing in the moment, it wasn't a magic cure for every unforgiving thought I've ever had. That's what I was unconsciously seeking. This now seems like magical thinking and far from the solid ground of reality. The problem with being a seeker is we're always seeking. We're never there. We're never content. Our sights are set on a vision of the future and whatever we seek seems to constantly elude us. By it's very nature, seeking is unfulfilling.

Once I truly understood that my lifetime habit of seeking, only evoked an unsatisfactory yearning within me, I woke up. Now when I find myself in seeking mode I intuitively know it's time to slow down and to allow myself to just be. A happy life, which to me means enjoying my experience and having a positive impact on the people around me, can be simple. We tend to make being happy much more difficult than it is.

When I work with my clients, I notice how they often bring a problem or question to a coaching session and usually by the end of our conversation they have a completely fresh perspective on the problem. Not only does the problem either dissolve or look solvable, there's a calming ripple effect which spills over into whatever else is going on in their life. Other problems disappear or look easy to handle, as a result of what they've seen when exploring the initial problem. George Pransky, one of my teachers, says, this understanding is like penicillin. It goes where it's needed. Unlike traditional coaching, where in the past I would help a client reach a specific goal in a linear fashion, this feels much more spontaneous and playful. I'm now able to help facilitate the client's awareness of their own connection to infinite creative potential. Not surprisingly, this makes business and life look a whole lot simpler both for me and the client.

Showing someone how their inner-game works and what's going on behind the scenes when they perform well, is like giving them the key to their success. The key effortlessly unlocks doors in our mind. It's the understanding of transforming the formless into form. Since I was a young child I've been fascinated with the concept of the spiritual nature of our human experience. I was often frustrated because no matter how many spiritual books I read, I couldn't see beyond the techniques and rituals so often presented as the key to enlightenment. I didn't know how it worked, so I spent a lot of time falling in and out of a wonderful feeling. I still had no clue how to get more out of my own software. I remember even as a young child, lying on the grass in the park, staring up at the clear, blue sky with a sense of pure wonder at the beauty of it all. I knew I was part of something much bigger than my little self. Now I have the understanding of how life unfolds in the simplest way - I can help people to tap into the giant pool of infinite possibilities. It's transformative and incredibly practical too.

After even one conversation, people new to my work, often share shifts in their productivity and performance. They feel a subtle shift although they might not be able to pinpoint what it is. On a practical level, it may look like they're suddenly able to get on with their business, project or life without procrastinating or worrying. In some instances, clients have been trying to create something they really want, for years. They've been getting in their own way by not understanding how the ebb and flow of creativity works. When I point to the nature of flow, suddenly the water looks clear and optimism returns. There's nothing to do, but so much to see.

PLAYING THE GAME

When we see life as a game, living feels lighter. Whatever happened in our past, we can choose to begin a new game without dragging our old losses on to the board. They mean nothing unless we think about them and give them meaning. Our past really only exists when we think of it. Trauma can only haunt us when we travel back mentally into past events. We all do this from time to time, in different ways. We torture ourselves. It can be as common as being lost in thought about the past, right through to Post Traumatic Stress Disorder or other mental 'disorders.' We all have mental health within us. The more we look towards our wellbeing rather than try to fix what we fear is broken, the more we access it.

This is why we often seek distraction when we feel disturbed. When we're engaged in the present moment, nothing else exists. This is a beautiful space to live in. Living fearlessly is about seeing this space within us. No striving or stress is required.

One of my first big insights through this understanding was about getting out of my own way. Some insights hit us like a force of nature and the ground shifts beneath our feet. As a result I found myself showing up differently without any concentrated effort. What I saw looked different and so I responded differently. I saw clearly how other people's insecurities weren't about me and so I didn't need to try to manage them. It turns out this can transform our entire experience of life. Repeatedly, I see more about how we get in our own way and the negative impact it has.

I first noticed this tendency years ago when working with people in business. The best tool in my kit to help people to break through their 'blocks,' usually involved motivation. Have you tried motivating people for a living? It can be exhausting work. This is because people can't really be motivated to do what they don't want to do. Much of the coaching profession works from the misunderstanding of helping clients to be accountable to their coach so they can make themselves do what they don't want to do. It's ridiculous when you think about it.

The Power Of Natural Motivation

I've never been terribly effective for long at helping people do what they don't want to do. It always seemed like such a waste of effort and energy. Why spend our precious life doing work, or being with people we don't want to be with? We can be the best motivators in the world but people run out of steam when they're not operating from their natural motivation. Natural motivation is like a bubbling stream, deep within each of us. Have you noticed there's no limit to our enthusiasm for doing what we want to do? The so called, 'resistance,' starts when we make ourselves do what we think we should do. I battled with the 'want' versus 'should' for many years. When we understand how our minds work, we follow through on what we truly want to do because we're not so easily fooled by our thoughts and feelings.

There's an ebb and flow to our experience of life which makes sense when we understand we're working with the giant pool of infinite creative potential. The giant pool is always open but sometimes it feels like an ebb rather than a flow. We can swim against the flow but most people don't manage for long because willpower isn't an unlimited resource. The ebb is part of the flow which cuts out a whole lot of swimming right there. We're always in flow because it's all the flow of life. We can allow ourselves to float in the pool.

I can be extremely tenacious and in some instances I wish I'd given up sooner. Our attachment to a goal can blind us to reality and to our highest good. When we've cultivated a mindset of 'do or die,' we can be like children determined to eat an ice-cream. In popular motivational mindset this is lauded as the goldmine attitude. I used to respect this way of thinking and so I aimed to be even more determined. As I already had a tendency to be rebellious and stubborn, looking back, I don't think this was particularly helpful. When we really want something, not much gets in our way of trying to have it. This can be wonderful and self-destructive at the same time. It depends on the situation. If we believe we need a specific outcome to be happy, it's usually an indication of suffering and struggle on the horizon.

> 'Our greatest weakness lies in giving up. The most certain way to succeed is always to try just one more time.'
>
> — THOMAS A. EDISON

In the past I would have been temporarily fired up when reading this quote. Now I see the idea of never giving up, as sometimes unhelpful. It depends on our level of understanding in the moment and our unique situation. In the case of Edison, his tenacity proved successful. In reality, if he hadn't continuously changed his approach and played with new creative ideas, it probably wouldn't have. There seems to be an element of giving up, letting go and allowing, involved in creating from the formless into form. This can't be taken into account in a one line quote. It's a good example of how the common misunderstanding of how success is achieved, can be perpetuated as a prescription.

Being determined doesn't mean we'll be successful. The world doesn't owe us success. Chipping away at the same fruitless dream for many years, whilst perhaps romantic, is no guarantee of the result we desire. I can be like a dog with a bone when I want something. However when the bone is dry, I've learned it's wise to move on. Prescriptions can be so misleading and even dangerous. People want certainty, and as such are easily led into believing such a concept exists. The only certainty lies in universal truth. Circumstances, personalities and situations, change and shift like the weather. I'm not sure there's one right way to do anything. We can all achieve many different outcomes in numerous ways and when we unhook ourselves from thinking there's a right way, there's more freedom to create what we want in a way which makes sense to us.

We don't know what's on the cards, even though many people can be very upset when they hear this. We tend to want to believe we can control and manipulate our future. Once we see it's beyond our ability, life becomes simpler. The weight of the world and the responsibility of trying to control everything, drops from our shoulders. If we don't need to be superman or woman and save the world, we can show up and play the game of life or business full out and fearlessly. When we see there's nothing to lose but our ego, conversely we more easily draw on our innate superpowers. And this unlimited power is fuelled by the inner spark which runs through us all. It's naturally powered like solar energy. We don't need motivating or empowering by others even if we think we do. This is incredibly liberating.

FULL OUT AND FEARLESS COACHING QUESTIONS

- Do you invest a lot of energy trying to make yourself do what you think you should, when you know in your heart you don't want to do it?
- Have you noticed how much easier it is to take action in a way you feel inspired to?
- Have you ever gone after something in a playful way because you thought the chances of attaining it, were slim?

- Can you see how different your experience is when you're not attached to a right way, and instead reinvent the game plan as you see what's needed in the moment?

Everything I'm pointing towards is already at work in our lives. When we begin to understand how it works, the game of life is easier to play. We can choose to play more games, knowing there's less riding on the outcome. Whilst most of us take our experience of life very seriously, it's seldom as serious as we like to think. Decisions can feel like a matter of life and death, but they rarely are. Many decisions are made when feeling insecure. We long to stop thinking about our 'problem,' and think we have to make a decision. Once we make a decision we may feel temporary relief. It's not because of the decision but because we've let it go and stopped thinking about it. When the decision wasn't made from a grounded place, the chances are we'll be thinking about it again soon.

We can't force our intuition to guide us to a place of knowing. It's wise to be patient and let the answer come to us. This can be particularly frustrating for high achieving action takers because there's nothing to do. Achievers usually get their highs from taking action and crossing items off their to-do list. Living Fearlessly is a more intuitive way of working with the flow of life which is already unfolding.

I'm not saying never to do things we don't feel like doing. We probably all sometimes have activities and tasks we're not in the mood to do. I see a difference between pushing through in the short-term and making our self do something we don't want to do over the long-term.

In the example of me writing this book; I'm inspired to write the book and I feel naturally motivated. Nobody needed to get me in the mood or tell me it's a good idea. I love books and mostly love writing them. This doesn't mean there aren't days where I don't feel like writing. There may be a day where I have a preference to lie around doing nothing and I may choose to honour it. If the same preference arises when I have a deadline I want to honour more than lying around, I'll probably write even if I'm not in the mood. However, when possible I've noticed it's usually more productive to work to my own ebb and flow.

When we override our built-in safety setting, by making ourselves work when we're unwell or tired, the results aren't usually great. Movement doesn't always equal quality. It seems more productive to follow our own flow but it's also very helpful to know we can work or produce even when we don't feel like it. The less busy thinking we have about what we're doing, generally, the clearer the channel to do whatever we want to do.

It doesn't seem either sustainable or enjoyable to whip ourselves into taking action over a long period of time in a way we don't want to. We all have preferences. Personally I'd rather not have to do errands, administrative tasks, cleaning and other necessary household activities I see as boring minutiae. I used to be very strict about planning and setting up my life and business systems so I could protect myself from the things I didn't want to do. I thought this was freedom, and in some ways it is helpful. Whilst I still prefer not to do these things, I'm no longer under the illusion that the activity I'm engaged in must determine my experience in the moment. When I had to clean the house recently because my highly efficient cleaner was sick, I noticed how easy it was once I threw myself into it.

This is common sense and we all know it but we can really rile ourselves up by thinking about how much we don't want to do something. Ego loves a good pity party. In truth, I can clean the house and indulge a lot of muddled, painful thinking about why I shouldn't have to. The chances are the cleaning won't go very smoothly because I'm not present and I'll hate it even more. Or I can accept it's something I want done and get on with it. I saw clearly it's always possible to have a horrible or a beautiful experience of cleaning the house, once I surrendered to the reality of what was in front of me.

A client shared with me how when we first started working together she'd hated doing a particular task in her business and had spent a lot of time thinking about what a problem it was. She shared how recently she's stopped procrastinating about getting the task done. She has been given more of it but to her great surprise has begun to enjoy it. This blew her mind as you might imagine. It's always possible for us to have a different experience of everyone and everything when we drop our stale ideas of who and what they are.

WE HAVE THE CAPACITY TO HANDLE WHATEVER LIFE THROWS AT US

When we understand our experience is always filtered through our personal lens, we hold the key to true mental freedom. We live in the feeling of our thinking all of the time. We're free to indulge our moods or to let them go. We're also free to fully feel our emotions without judging ourselves. What's rich about this depth of feeling, is we feel more alive. The need to protect ourselves from our emotions, naturally falls away when we see the truth of how we're designed to cope with whatever life throws at us. We don't always like it; but we do have the capacity to handle it.

The more we see the truth of how life already works, the more we notice how we get in our own way. When we give ourselves permission to do what we want, we become effortlessly productive. We get savvy to when to stop and when to push on. Goals give us direction but we don't need to kill ourselves fulfilling them. They are helpful until they're not. Years ago in a seminar, before I understood any of what I'm sharing in this book, the motivational trainer said,

'I'll get to the top of the mountain or I'll die trying.'

It was well meant as a rallying cry to beat the odds. I remember feeling very emotional and excited by those words. Now I see it as an insecure foundation to build a business and life upon. Why would we want to kill ourselves for a business anyway? This is the type of hyped-up motivational training which promotes suffering when people don't reach their goals. Goals are brilliant as something to aim for but we don't need to die on the mountain to be worthy of success.

When we're attached to the form of how something turns out, we limit our creativity and resources because we're not open to fresh solutions and unexpected opportunities. We're not our work or business; our potential is much greater. One, or even many opportunities may not work out but something new always awaits. We'll never see the infinite possibilities when we're blinkered and attached to what our ego thinks it needs in order to survive.

GIVING UP ISN'T FOR LOSERS

I used to think giving up was for losers. I would push through trying to make things happen which on reflection really didn't seem to want to happen. I had the misunderstanding that sheer willpower and a 'can do' attitude was what was needed and so I cultivated more of it.

I read hundreds of books and listened to audios and attended seminars on how to be bullet proof and never to give up. Giving up had a real stigma to it in my empowered circles. The problem with this is that life doesn't really work this way. Even when we think we've created something through our own tenacity and willpower, it's not the whole story. There are other factors at play which we can't and don't control even if we'd like to think we do. This in turn sets us up for suffering when the dice don't land in our favour. We beat ourselves up thinking it's all on us. Conversely, when we think we made something happen all on our own, our egos inflate. We revel in the gratification, until the next ego-fuelled challenge shows up to test us and we begin all over again.

This is illusory and casts us out on the winds of fortune. It looks as if by being empowered we're in control. When we glimpse the truth of how reality works, we're free to show up and do what makes sense to us. Sometimes it goes as we think it should and sometimes it doesn't. From this space we can access clarity on demand because we're free to try. We're free to play full out and fearless. We're no longer so afraid. We're also free to give up. Giving up isn't fatal or final. Humans are a bit like cockroaches. We find a way under, over, or around.

Giving up or letting go when we don't know what to do isn't weakness; it's wisdom. Have you ever noticed how the minute you give up on a tricky problem or you walk away, something seems to shift? This is a bit like the back burner I referred to in the last chapter. We may receive a phone call out of the blue, or bump into someone we haven't seen in years who can help us. I don't understand the metaphysics of this but I've certainly experienced it in my life, many times. Have you? What I'm pointing to, are the principles behind this phenomenon which are reliable and predictable.

When we give up on something we've been trying so hard to do, we allow our self the mental space to see our problem with new eyes and come back to it with fresh thinking. Sometimes we see the problem doesn't even need solving anymore. It fixes itself or we get an insight; a new idea on how to solve the problem. The solution wasn't there before in our consciousness. We didn't have it in our mind before but when we give up, we allow space for something new to come in.

There's a story I heard from a colleague about an aerospace company which was exposed to the principles I share in my work. They began to take the idea of 'giving up' to a whole new level. After seeing the power of giving up they would walk away from their desk. They would go home and take time out, instead of continuing to tackle problems. We're talking aerospace here so I'm guessing these were not simple problems. They would allow themselves the mental space for something new to come through and the new modus operandi became 'how quickly can you give up?' These smart technical geeks are walking around asking each other, 'Have you given up yet?' If this is helpful for aerospace engineers, perhaps we can learn a thing or two for our daily problem solving.

We can let go and trust the infinite creative potential will give us what we need. This is why it can feel so comforting to pray.

It's as if we're handing over or letting go of a problem which is beyond our control. It helps take it off our mind but also feels as if we're doing something about it.

There seems to be an element of allowing things to unfold. We can give up or let go but if we don't allow, then we stop the flow of whatever wants to happen. I see allowing or accepting as being at peace with what is. It seems to me a little bit like, when we're engaged in work and we've got a lot going on. We try to move forward and suddenly something happens to slow us down and take us out of the game. Perhaps we're unwell or an unexpected commitment comes up.

When we're in a space of allowing, we're open to the unknown. For instance, when someone wants to help, what might happen if we accept the offer? What if we don't close people and opportunities down so quickly? I do this sometimes. I often have a definite idea of what I want to do. I'm a fast action taker and sometimes I'm not open to hearing what other people want to tell me. I've noticed that asking more about what someone wants to say, can really lead me to some interesting places. They could be talking about something completely different to what I could previously envisage. When we see the value in slowing down, we don't miss ideas and resources which may help us. What might we allow to come through to support us with our business, work or life?

SAYING YES AND NO

Recently I was reading 'The Year of Yes,' by Shonda Rhimes, the creator of one of my all-time favourite shows, 'Grey's Anatomy.' The book reminded me of 'Feel the Fear and Do it Anyway' in some respects because the philosophy is to fight resistance and treat fear as a tangible block. Understanding what I do now about how fear works, this approach seems less helpful. However, I still loved the book because it's inspiring. Shonda says yes to invitations which she was too terrified to say yes to before, or which she never even contemplated saying yes to in the past. It's a bit like allowing herself to play in the unknown. What could it be like to say yes to something which we'd usually automatically say no to? What could it be like to say no to something we usually say yes to? This isn't a strategy where I'm advising, 'Say yes to everything or say no to everything.' That's not what I'm pointing to at all.

This is why I love 'Living Fearlessly.' It's so fluid and flexible in the moment to what shows up. We might say no to something today. We might say yes to something tomorrow. We might say yes and no within the space of ten minutes. We may change our mind. It's all fine. We free ourselves by giving ourselves permission to say no when we feel in our gut we don't want to say yes. Usually we may say yes to please people, or because we're worried about what it says about us if we say no.

What if we say yes to life, more? Because, what the hell, why not? We can try something new. It might exceed our expectations beyond anything we ever imagined. Or we might hate it and never choose to say yes to it again. Either way we're free to choose. Our personalities are not as fixed as we think. We have the free will to choose and change.

———

HERE'S A SUMMARY OF THE KEY POINTS IN THIS CHAPTER:

- We tend to make being happy much more difficult than it is.
- Understanding how the inner-game works is the key to our success. The key effortlessly unlocks doors in our mind.
- When we see life as a game, living feels lighter.
- So called 'resistance,' starts when we make ourselves do what we think we should do.
- Giving up or letting go when we don't know what to do isn't weakness; it's wisdom.
- Living Fearlessly is a more intuitive way of working with the flow of life which is already unfolding.

There's an 'insight' space below to journal any new thoughts that come through as you read:

_____

_____

_____

Next we'll explore loving fearlessly and the ripple effect on our relationships, work and the world.

10

LOVING FEARLESSLY

'My love is like a red, red rose; its fragrance fills the air; it guides me to a place of light; instead of dark despair.'

— Sydney Banks

Love is the antidote to fear. This is why I want to dedicate the final chapter of 'Living Fearlessly' to sharing what I've seen about the true nature of love. Love dissolves fear effortlessly. Where there is love, there's no fear. The two cannot simultaneously exist. When we understand the true nature of love, we're more likely to be loving, to ourselves and to others.

People naturally become less reactive and more loving as they go deeper into this fearless space. When the mind settles, the default setting is love. When we seek to understand and lead with goodwill, not judgement, we access a pure, loving connection. When we see our wellbeing doesn't ride on people's behaviour, we're open to a new experience. The chemistry we create with another human being is unique. In each encounter we always have the choice to show up as love, which encourages harmony. When we show up with judgement, it tends to promote discord.

It's a great relief to see we don't have to be attached to how someone behaves. When we allow people the freedom to be whoever they are in the moment, we release ourselves from mental prison. We no longer feel quite so compelled to immediately jump in to put them straight. Our inner wisdom guides us in a more loving direction when we recognise and follow it. It's another load off our shoulders when we see our relationships can be much simpler than we've been conditioned to believe. We don't need to manage or fix them.

We Construct Our Personalities

I've been guilty of reactive behaviour throughout much of my life. In my enthusiasm to understand and to be understood, I've often been over-zealous in communicating my point of view. Some of this insecurity was fuelled from feeling as though I didn't speak up enough as a young child. If I were to ask any of my family if I was timid, they'd probably laugh. In truth, I don't know, but I suspect I wasn't as invisible as I've led myself to believe. It's a great example of how we construct our personalities, as well as those of everyone in our world, through our thoughts.

I see 'Rachel,' through different lenses, depending on the state of mind I'm in when I think of her. I can see her through my loving lens and there are no problems. I feel compassion for her humanity and can see she's doing the best she can, given her level of consciousness in the moment. When it looks like a good idea to judge her through my critical lens, Rachel can be quite a handful. She often needs fixing because she's not quite good enough as she is.

When I was a teenager my father occasionally shook his head in despair and pronounced me a rebel without a cause. I think I knew I'd find a worthy cause so it never worried me much. Fortunately, I now know, whatever lens I use, my experience of Rachel is completely made of thought. Sometimes I forget. When I do, I think it's a very serious business to make sure Rachel gets what she thinks she needs. I've spent a lifetime speaking up, to compensate for my belief that I wasn't heard or acknowledged fully as a child. This also comes through in my tendency to defend those I perceive as the underdog.

Rachel can argue both sides of a case with conviction and sometimes forgets why she's arguing at all. She loves to see all viewpoints and sometimes feels irritated when others don't or won't. I can laugh at myself now, knowing 'myself' is completely made up, and can be changed any time. I find this very freeing. I'm free to lose my temper, to let go of anger quickly and to apologise without a second thought. I have less respect for being right. There's no right. It's just my perception of what's happening. It makes life and relationships seem much more fulfilling and loving. We are truly free spirits when we let go of who we think we are.

The way I used to live was exhausting. When we think we have to control outcomes, it's as if we're trying to control the universe. It's quite a job. When we attempt to control circumstances, we're usually in the business of trying to control the people around us too. Part of the job description is to make them do more of the things we think we need them to do in order for us to be okay.

This sounds really selfish, but it's how many people unconsciously operate. It's not because we're inherently selfish. It's because we're afraid of not knowing what's going to happen. We're scared of the unknown, so we try to overcompensate by performing more than our role. I see our role as showing up, and being present to what we can contribute. When we're open and connected we're like conduits. Instead, we tend to go a step further and say, 'I should have said that to them, and why didn't I say this, and maybe if I say that next time, they'll do this.'

IT'S NOT OUR JOB TO MANAGE THE UNIVERSE

I'm sure that scenario sounds familiar to most people. We've probably all had a similar conversation running through our minds many times throughout our lives. Perhaps even in the last few days. We've all done it. We all do it sometimes. When we see it's not our job to manage the universe; things are going to work out however they work out, a lot of extraneous thinking drops away. What's left in its place? A beautiful, quiet space where we can really be our true fearless selves.

We're free to do the things we want to do; to be fearless, knowing we're okay, whatever the outcome. It's one of my favourite facets of this understanding of how reality works. I often forget the fearless space is always available to us. I still get lost in my fast, insecure thinking. It's an old habit. I'm used to worrying. It's also the human condition. At some point I wake up again and reconnect with the most wonderful feeling of peace and love inside me. I know it's all unfolding as it's meant to and I was temporarily lost in a nightmare of my own creation. The difference for me these days is, I know it's okay to feel okay. However, a casual observer could well conclude that I occasionally do my absolute best to give myself a hard time. Many of my clients have reported similar realisations of knowing they're okay and wondering if it's too good to be true.

If we knew and never forgot that we're made of pure love there'd be no need for work like this. There would be no reason to write, 'Living Fearlessly,' because our natural state is fearless. There would be no need for transformation coaching because we'd all be living fearlessly. There wouldn't be any uncovering of love required because we'd all operate in love all of the time.

The thought created version of us I portrayed earlier, may sound a bit odd but we do the same with others too. Our children, partner, parents, friends and acquaintances, are all perceived through our personal thinking. If they were a fixed entity we'd either love, like or hate them consistently. What really happens is we can feel love for them one minute and anger the next. We can feel compassion for one person and feel insecure with another. It's nothing to do with the person. I've pointed to the principle of thought, throughout the book because we experience everything and everyone, through our thinking, from the inside-out.

'How a person seems to show up for us is intimately connected to how we choose to show up for them.' Marianne Williamson, Return to Love

THE PERSONALITY OF OUR RELATIONSHIPS

This is why some people love us and others have no time for us. It's why some days we get on well with someone, and others we have no patience for them. We're all living in our thought created reality and our state of mind fluctuates constantly. The personality of our relationships fluctuates with it.

Hopefully, we've travelled together far enough in this book for you to glimpse the truth of what I'm sharing. I understand it can be confusing to discover we have so much freedom to choose how we show up in our relationships. It can feel easier to blame others for how we feel, but it never works that way. Our thoughts about another person's words or actions are what create our feelings. We can't choose what we think so there's nothing to do about it. But it's liberating to see our feelings for what they are. We feel our thoughts and this provides a reliable feedback system of what's going on in our head.

The great news is that people aren't as fixed as we thought. We are not wholly good or bad, but loving, insecure and everything in-between. This changes moment to moment, given our state of mind, which fluctuates like the temperature. We like to call this phenomenon of the changing barometer, moods or mood swings. We may accuse people of being moody. We're all moody, but some moods such as the happiness mood is popular and socially acceptable. When dark thoughts strike and we feel down, we're labelled moody, but really we're just experiencing another note in the symphony of the grand human experience.

Sometimes we feel sadness and it shows on our face or comes through in our voice. In society we're encouraged to always pretend to be happy and to put a brave face on our feelings. This can be quite a challenge for someone going through a difficult time and who's feeling intense sadness. They may withdraw from company for this very reason. If it was more acceptable to show our feelings even when they're not happy ones, we'd be less likely to think there's something wrong with us when we feel sad. We'd also be able to move through our emotions quicker because our minds would naturally settle and we'd be restored to our innate mental health with no intervention. When we feel judged or we judge ourselves for feeling a certain way, the feeling often deepens and we see it as a real problem needing to be fixed.

When we're having problems with a relationship, it's common to blame the other person for what they did, which we think upset us. This would make perfect sense if we didn't only ever experience what they do, through our own filtered thinking. This is why when someone says something to us and we feel hurt, a friend may not see it as hurtful. They may have a different perception of what was said and don't assign the same meaning to it as we do. Sometimes large groups of people agree on the same meaning and so it's easy to be tricked into thinking the meaning comes from what was said or done. It never does; it comes from what we think about it and how it was projected in our virtual reality show called life. No one has the power to make us feel a certain way. When we don't understand the thought-feeling system, it really seems as though they do.

We are enough. We are worthy. We are made of love. If only everyone knew this there wouldn't be so much hatred and fear. Imagine if we were taught about how we perceive our reality at school. Imagine living in a world where children are taught about the nature of love and how they already have everything they need within them, to live wonderful lives. If we were all pointed to our innate well-being and mental health as the default from the day we were born, it would be such a different way of being. Instead, we're usually pointed to why we need to be fearful and why we'll never be enough. We're told we're different and separate from other people or other groups. If we're from strict religious backgrounds we're often shamed and told what terrible sinners we are.

My mother and her four sisters were all convent educated and as part of the tradition I attended a Catholic school until the age of ten. We were briskly marched to church, in pairs, at least three times a week. My family on my mother's side, with whom I lived until the age of ten, lived by their own rules. My father had no time for church. But for some reason it was deemed a good idea my cousin and I go to religious schools. Perhaps they secretly feared they weren't up to the task of guarding our tender, young souls. My mother and her sisters had probably endured more than their fair share of devout obedience training by the time they were released from the convent. They were wilful and a little wild so I imagine it wasn't an easy job for the nuns to keep them in line.

Between the ages of five and ten I would attend Confession several times a week. I remember earnestly trying to come up with 'good sins' to admit to the priest in the confessional. Knowing my competitive streak it's no surprise to me that I took it to the level of inventing the best sin. I'd come up with all types of creative sins. My goal, as I recall, was to have something to admit to, which was sufficiently sinful. It wouldn't go well if I had the gall to try and appear innocent, but it mustn't be so bad I would be sitting there for hours with too heavy a penance. As it was, I'd need to sit on the hard bench for quite some time, reciting Hail Marys with my set of delicate, white and silver rosary beads. It's quite a challenge for a young child to sit patiently for long periods, contemplating their sinful nature. My fall-back sin was to admit to refusing to switch the electric blanket on when my grandmother asked me to. I'm not sure I ever committed this evil sin but occasionally, my imagination failed me and I had to come up with a sin on the spot. My sin, if there was one, would be more likely to be lying about the content of my sin. This seems like a ridiculously comical routine now but at the time it was very serious indeed.

LOVING OURSELVES IS OUR BIRTHRIGHT

I used to think loving oneself more was a nice idea, but wondered how to practice it. Now I see it's our birthright. We're not born with feelings of unworthiness. If we're told we're unworthy many times, and believe that not feeling worthy or good enough is truth, it becomes our reality. When we see how our worthiness is also a thought created construct, it's easier to love ourselves. We see our judgement of ourselves isn't permanent and we can drop the judgement when a new thought shows up. When we think unloving thoughts about ourselves and we're in the habit of taking our thinking seriously, we feel bad. It really is this simple.

The key to raising the consciousness of the planet is to know how we each experience our own reality. It begins with us. There's a ripple effect of love when we see our true nature is love and we have nowhere to go to get more of it. When feelings of unworthiness surface, we lose our footing and the ground feels shaky. We feel insecure and that's when we lash out. We look for our self-worth in other people and get confused when it's not there. Seeking our value through the eyes of our partner is not only unfair to them but it's also impossible to find. The only place we can truly love ourselves is from within. Once we experience this truth, not intellectually, but in a real life situation, we know we're okay whatever happens with our relationships.

Of course we have preferences about who we'd like to spend our lives with. We enjoy free will to choose who we want to spend time with. But there also appears to be an element of what's on the cards for us. We don't know what will happen in the future but we can create drama when we act from insecurity not love. When we think we're not having our needs met, it can feel as if we need to take urgent action to fix our relationships. We may feel the need to make decisions and to move fast. There are times when it does make sense to make decisions about leaving relationships or changing our situation, but most people make them when they're in a low, reactive mood. This is when we're most ill-equipped to make sound decisions.

Have you noticed how trying to connect with someone when they're angry or in a low mood is much more difficult than when they're calm? It's precisely at these times we tend to jump in and tackle situations. We want to be able to stop persecuting ourselves with our dark thoughts and so we feel compelled to take urgent action. This is how many divorces and relationship break-ups, spiral out of control. Both parties feel insecure and try to make decisions from shaky ground where neither has clarity. This is also how wars and conflicts escalate.

When there's no goodwill present in a relationship it can feel as though there are insurmountable problems to deal with. This is why counselling doesn't save most marriages. People show up with what they see as problems and their partner is usually the number one problem in their mind. Unless the counsellor is able to facilitate the understanding for each person to see the innocent nature of their partner's experience, lasting transformation is unlikely to occur. Couples can spend months or even years working hard to change their own and their partner's behaviour on a surface level, but get nowhere. People usually don't want to change their behaviour to obtain approval. We want to feel loved and accepted as we are. When we feel compassion for someone, they're much more likely to try to change whatever bothers us. Or, when our insecure judgement drops away we see they don't need to change after all. This is why after an argument, when goodwill is restored, we often laugh at our own ridiculous behaviour. We see we've once again been deluded by our ego and everything looks different, even when nothing has changed. The ability to laugh at our human frailty is a soothing, restorative gift.

When we're guided to look upstream of the surface behavioural 'problems,' we're able to see the nature of each other's insecurity. From this point of compassion; goodwill and love naturally enter the conversation. This isn't to say relationships won't end, even when we understand how our experience works. This understanding explains how humans tick and what's really going on. It doesn't mean we can't make choices about what we want, but it means we can make them from a more sane, loving place.

In the same way it seems easier to be loving to ourselves when we understand the transient nature of thought, and how powerful it can feel, we also begin to naturally feel more compassion for others. Occasionally I used to think my daughters needed sorting out. In my mind, sometimes their behaviour was problematic and I thought it my job as their mother to help them. Have you ever tried getting the better of a teenager? You usually lose, or you win the argument but lose their goodwill. These days I'd rather lose the argument and keep their goodwill. I'm not advocating we be pathetic and let people walk all over us. It's just that the less seriously we take people's insecurity, the less it seems to be a problem. The quicker it blows over. When we lead with ego, not love, we lose our connection. My relationships with my daughters have improved, rather than deteriorated, through what are traditionally seen as the tricky teenage years. No one wants to be fixed or put straight, whatever their age. It may give us satisfaction to do it to someone, but it usually backfires.

WE WANT WHAT WE WANT

We never change people's minds by bullying them and this is true of our own too. We want what we want. We can talk ourselves into doing things we don't want, but we all have an inner knowing. We want what we want, and when we quieten down enough, we know exactly what it is. If we don't know, it's usually best not to do anything. We can let the thought storm settle and the dark clouds pass which they will. Once we're thinking clearly we all know what or who we want but it may be very inconvenient and we wish it wasn't so. Life doesn't usually unfold in the way we planned. At some point we settle down enough to act on what we want, with love and compassion, not insecurity. When we act from love, even complex situations transform in ways we couldn't possibly imagine when examined through fearful thinking.

Love can feel like an addiction. When we're addicted to the feeling which love evokes in us, we may use it as a distraction from other thoughts and feelings. I've noticed how many of us live in the illusion of needing our lover, and everyone else we love, to behave a certain way for us to be okay. What I've seen deeply about love through conversations with my clients and through my own experience, is that true love feels pure and beautiful. Love isn't needy. Pure love isn't negotiated in a 'I'll love you if you do this or be like this,' way. Love transcends our own insecurities in a way that being addicted to the feeling of being wanted or loved can't. When we don't see the difference, it's common to feel as if we're being triggered by the behaviour of our loved ones. It's not possible to be triggered. No one has the ability to make us feel anything.

PURE LOVE IS UNCONDITIONAL

Suddenly, what felt like pure love now seems like oxygen. It feels as though we really need a certain person to love us or we might die. And most love songs perpetuate this myth. One of my favourite love songs is 'Without You' by Nilsson. He sings, 'I can't live if living is without you.' I can still listen to the song and revel in the feeling but the difference is I now know it's not truth. When we're addicted to the feeling of being wanted, life can feel very difficult because our wellbeing becomes dependent on someone else. That's fine when they're doing what we want but what about when they're not? Pure love is unconditional. We know we love someone unconditionally when we love them whatever they do. Their highest good is a priority for us rather than our own insecure needs.

I don't mean to suggest we play the role of a victim of love. We don't decide who we love, we fall in love, but we can choose to be in a relationship or not. We can choose to leave or stay and we can choose how much we invest in our relationships. I often hear women say things like 'I'll stand by him no matter what.'

It's as if it's some kind of sacrifice, but really when we love someone we just love them. When our love doesn't come from our need to feel worthy, we're effortlessly loving. No fixing of one another is necessary.

When we don't know that our feelings of love are subject to our mood in the moment, relationships can feel like hard work. Our moods change frequently and our thoughts are as unpredictable as the wind. If we're living out fearful fantasies about why he or she did what they did and what it means about us, we're caught up in addiction to the feeling of love and approval. When we see for ourselves, love isn't conditional on someone's behaviour, we're free to love fearlessly. If someone else's behaviour doesn't determine our self-worth as a wife, husband, lover, parent or friend, we're free to love them with our whole being. We're free to feel our emotions deeply, knowing the feelings will pass and they can't damage us. We can love, laugh, disagree or argue, safe in the knowledge that our mental wellbeing is intact. Feelings evaporate. The more we see our true nature is love, the less we need to protect or defend ourselves.

When we've been hurt or feel we've had our heart broken, it's natural to want to raise our defences. It may seem like common sense to avoid being vulnerable again because we think we can't then be hurt. The problem is, when we hold back from feeling whatever wants to be felt, we miss out on feeling other emotions deeply. When we're guarding ourselves from being hurt we're unable to love fearlessly. We attempt to deaden our ability to love, in our effort to protect ourselves from pain. As we begin to appreciate how resilient we are, a defence mechanism seems less useful, even if such a device could protect us from feeling. In reality, we may try to close down our ability to feel love but there's no way I know of for humans to permanently turn off their feelings. We are spiritual beings having a human experience and part of the human condition is to feel emotion.

When we feel bad we can let the emotion have its way with us. We soon see that thought can't kill us even if it feels like we're dying of pain. It's okay to feel sad. It's human, and completely normal. I'm not saying we won't feel hurt or abandoned in certain situations. I can however guarantee that at some point, a fresh, new thought will find its way into our mind. This usually happens once we settle down and accept what is. We can let emotion pass through us. We also have the capacity to observe our thoughts. But for our judgement about how we feel, we're okay, no matter who loves us. It's great when we get what we want but we can recover when we don't, even if we don't like the experience. Love is intact within us, unless we mess with the default settings by indulging our thinking about how we need someone else to validate us. As soon as we let go of our need to control, we're free to love fearlessly.

When we're loving, we have access to the infinite power supply to impact others, by being present with them. When we're awake to our inner spark, our presence is so powerful, other people light up around us. Sometimes this is through a transformative conversation and at others we may be touched by the beautiful feeling in the silence between words. Silence really can be golden. We all have the capacity to be love conductors. Each spark of love we transmit, raises the consciousness of those around us. When we feel love, we are fearless.

———

HERE'S A SUMMARY OF THE KEY POINTS IN THIS
CHAPTER:

- In each encounter we always have the choice to show up as love.
- We construct our personalities, as well as those of everyone in our world, through our thoughts.
- We're not born with feelings of unworthiness. Loving ourselves is our birthright.
- Each mood we experience is like another note in the symphony of the grand human experience.
- We can create chaos when we act from insecurity not love.
- When we really see for ourselves, love isn't conditional on someone's behaviour, we're free to love fearlessly.
- We are spiritual beings having a human experience and part of the human condition is to feel emotion.

There's an 'insight' space below to journal any new thoughts that come through as you read:

_____

_____

_____

SHARING LIVING FEARLESSLY

If you've been impacted by this book I would be so grateful if you could leave a short review on Amazon or wherever you bought it. This will help more people to live fearlessly.

To help others who are trying to fight their fears, please recommend this book, or give a copy to someone you love.

I'd also love to hear from you, so if you'd like to share your living fearlessly insights, please email me at info@Rachelhenke.com or use the hashtag #livingfearlessly on social media.

Thank you so much for joining me.

Register for your missing chapter bonus video lesson where I share my Living Fearlessly Method to achieve what you want at https://www.livingfearlessly.co.uk/bonus

ACKNOWLEDGMENTS

I'm grateful to Nicola Bird and Michael Neill. If it weren't for you, I would still be seeking freedom in the wrong direction.

Thanks to Russell Cooper. Your contribution has made this book not only simpler to digest but significantly more impactful too.

I'm in awe of my daughter, Amy Henke's, geekery and design skills. This book and the companion Living Fearlessly website are indebted to you!

Thanks to all of my wonderful clients who have embarked on the fearless journey with me as their guide.

I'm blessed with family, friends and colleagues around the world who support me. There are too many to list but you know who you are. I love you.

And finally, thanks to all of my readers who take the time to read, share their insights and to recommend this book.

ABOUT THE AUTHOR

Rachel Henke is the Founder of Living Fearlessly, Transformation Coach and Bestselling Author of numerous books.

Breaking free of the job world upon relocating to a sleepy village in the UK, Rachel started her first business working from the breakfast bar around her two young daughters.

After 30 years of self-improvement, she has finally found the answers she was seeking.

Combined with her extensive business and transformative coaching expertise she helps her clients to move through fear so they can follow their dreams with confidence and ease.

Continue your fearless journey with Rachel at:
www.Livingfearlessly.co.uk/bonus
info@rachelhenke.com

ALSO BY RACHEL HENKE

The Niche Expert: Harness The Power Of The Internet To Attract
Perfect Clients, Publicity & Opportunities

The Freedom Solution: More Perfect Clients & Profits In Less Time

Made in the USA
San Bernardino, CA
22 November 2017